Davis, Terrell,
1972-

 TD.

$23.00

TD

TD
Dreams in Motion

Terrell Davis

WITH

ADAM SCHEFTER

FOREWORD BY

JOHN ELWAY

HarperCollins*Publishers*

HarperCollins books may be purchased for educational, business, or sales promotional use. For information please write: Special Markets Department, HarperCollins Publishers, Inc., 10 East 53rd Street, New York, NY 10022.

FIRST EDITION

Library of Congress Cataloging-in-Publication Data

Davis, Terrell, 1972–
    TD : dreams in motion / Terrell Davis, Adam Schefter.—1st ed.
     p. cm.
    ISBN 0-06-019282-8
     1. Davis, Terrell, 1972– . 2. Football players—United States—Biography.
    3. Denver Broncos (Football team). I. Schefter, Adam. II. Title.
GV939.D347A3 1998
796' .332'092—dc21
    [b]   98-34498

98 99 00 01 02 ❖/RRD 10 9 8 7 6 5 4 3 2 1

For Mom and Pops, one who's looking out for me and one who's looking down on me

—*Terrell Davis*

For Shirley and Jeffrey, my parents, my best friends

—*Adam Schefter*

CONTENTS

TERRELL DAVIS: AN APPRECIATION

BY JOHN ELWAY

When it comes to Sundays and game days, I try to keep a pretty good eye on everything going on around me. Wish I could say the same thing about my wife, Janet.

She sat through all the pre-game festivities, all the half-time entertainment and the Broncos' first-ever Super Bowl win at Qualcomm Stadium in San Diego last January, without realizing that Terrell Davis's mom, Mrs. Kateree Davis, was sitting right behind her the entire time.

Janet made up for it, though. Once the game was secure, our celebration was under way, and Janet did notice who was seated behind her, she turned around, hugged Mrs. Davis, and told her, "Your son allowed our dream to come true." I couldn't have said it much better myself.

Without Terrell, I don't think we would have won Super Bowl XXXII. The Green Bay Packers did a great job stopping the pass but they didn't stop the run. For us to rely on moving the ball through the air would have been difficult. As the second quarter proved, we had only 14 yards of total offense when Terrell missed the second quarter because of his migraine headache.

If Terrell hadn't come back, I'm not sure that our coach, Mike Shanahan, would have been able to stay with the game plan that had already produced 31 points for us. Fortunately, though, Terrell did, and so did our running game, our offensive attack, and our chances of winning.

Terrell was such a huge contributor not only in the Super Bowl, but all during the regular season and the playoffs. Anytime you have a guy who runs 1,750 yards during the regular season and another 581 during the postseason, it's pretty obvious how important he is. Even more important with Terrell—something a lot of people might not have always realized—was that it didn't matter whether we were scoring points all the time or not. What mattered was that we were able to chew the clock and win the field-position wars. With Terrell, we've won a lot of wars.

When Terrell first got to Denver back in 1995, the thing that I noticed about him right away was the way he walked, the bounce in his step. I knew he either had great speed or strong legs. And though Terrell's not super-fast, he is super-strong in his legs. He runs with power and has a great ability to break tackles.

In his first preseason with the Broncos, I saw him break all kinds of tackles. Still, I don't care whose looking good and what anybody's saying in the summer, you never know how good someone is until the real games start. But Terrell got out there in his first NFL game against the Buffalo Bills, had 20 carries for 70 yards and a touchdown, and he was very good. I thought to myself, "This guy's got a real chance to make it." I didn't realize he was also going to give me another shot to make it back to the Super Bowl.

Ever since his rookie season, Terrell has taken the pressure off me to throw on every down. Our offense has been better because people have had to worry about not only our passing game but also our running game. Even when it seemed to be an obvious passing down, say second-and–10, defenses couldn't tee off on me because Terrell could run the ball no matter what down it was, no matter how far we had to go.

Off the field, I haven't spent a whole lot of time around Terrell. I'm an older guy who's married and has four children; he's a younger guy who's single. Most of the time we spend together is at work, where he is a real down-to-earth person, a quality guy, someone who has strong morals and high standards, and lives up to those as a role model. That's one reason he's so popular around Denver and the rest of the NFL. Terrell's real.

The longer he continues to be successful, the more he will realize how tough popularity can be to handle. My philosophy has always been this: Every time you add a positive to your life, you're also going to add a negative. For example, if you sign a new contract, there's the added responsibility of taking care of that money. A lot of times those types of negatives beat on your conscience because you want to be able to do everything, but you can't. And eventually, it might wear you down mentally. That's one of the toughest things Terrell is going to face now and in the future.

The bottom line is, he has to make sure that football is his focus and that he continues to do what it takes to be the great football player he is. He cannot let anything or anyone distract him from what he's trying to accomplish—to become one of the best running backs in all of football. As it is, he is the best running back I have ever played with, there's no question about it, and he is one of the elite running backs in the game today. Personally? I wouldn't trade Terrell for anybody else in the league.

There's no question he has a chance to be one of the all-time greats. Look at where he is now compared to where every other running back was after his first three years in the league. After three seasons, Terrell has run for 4,405 yards. The only players in NFL history who ever ran for more during their first three years were the former Rams running back Eric Dickerson, who ran for 5,147, and the former Oiler and Saint Earl Campbell, who ran for 5,081.

I like a lot of things about Terrell as a player, but one of the things I love most about him is that he has gotten so much better so quickly. It's almost scary to think about how good he could be. I hope he keeps on going right at this rate. I hope he goes 15 more years, and makes a lot of future Bronco quarterbacks' jobs a lot easier, the way he has mine.

His legacy will come from continuing to do great things over time. The good thing with Terrell is, he's working hard in the off-season—lifting, taking care of himself. That type of attitude has helped me stay around and it's going to help him stay around, too.

Terrell's biggest challenges will be trying to stay healthy and performing at a high level over the long haul. He does that, he's going to make a lot more dreams come true.

—*John Elway*
May 12, 1998

INTRODUCTION

With the serious look of the attorney and certified public accountant that he is, Neil Schwartz, agent for Denver Broncos running back Terrell Davis, looked at me and posed a question that sounded as silly as it was naïve.

"When Terrell writes his book," he asked, "how'd you like to do it?"

This was almost two years ago, July 1996, way before anyone actually knew just how good Terrell was, as a person and a player. Terrell had just come off a rookie season in which he had come out of Georgia after running for 1,117 yards, his first bit of real recognition since he had earned the nickname "Boss Hogg" in his Pop Warner football days back in San Diego. He had just renegotiated his contract to a salary figure more appropriate to a first-round pick than the sixth-round pick he had been one year earlier. Terrell was a terrifically nice guy; it would make a good little story.

But a book? Books are supposed to be for handsome

young actors named Leonardo and championship-winning quarterbacks named John and wise old teachers named Morrie, not one-year wonders named Terrell.

"Sure," I told Schwartz, as diplomatically as possible. "Down the line, you guys ever want to do a book, I'm happy to help." I figured there was as much chance of a Terrell book as there was of a Bronco Super Bowl victory parade.

I was just another Davis doubter, the latest in a too-many-to-count series of them.

But then, in each of the next two years, Terrell ran for well over 1,000 yards and led the American Football Conference in rushing. Carrying the football and Denver, he ran the Broncos back into the Super Bowl. And once there, he scored a Super Bowl–record three rushing touchdowns, as well as Super Bowl XXXII Most Valuable Player honors.

Then came the Broncos' victory parade through downtown Denver last January, when Terrell sat atop a fire truck with more than 650,000 screaming fans saluting him like a superhero.

TD! TD! TD!

Like the Broncos, Terrell had gone from underdog to big dog, bringing his story and this autobiography to life. And last January, the night after the Broncos' Super Bowl parade, the phone in my apartment rang. It was a familiar voice, asking a question that now sounded neither silly nor naïve.

"Still interested in doing that book?" Schwartz asked.

But what I didn't know, and couldn't know until I had spent the blocks of time with Terrell that I did, was that his story would have been worth telling even if he had never been a Super Bowl hero. Terrell's excelling in football only provided him with a stage from which to tell his story. In my opinion, what Terrell has had to endure on a football field does not begin to match what he has had to endure off it. We knew Terrell had to overcome obstacles to get to the top of that fire truck. Up until now, we just had no idea how many.

This is the story of one person's struggle, one person's perseverance. It is a story that helps explain who the man is. And who Terrell Davis is—and I'm guessing here that I'm not telling any NFL defenses anything they didn't already know—is a man who is incredibly difficult to bring down.

Yet some people, for their own reasons, still like to take their shots. Just last May, at a fundraising party in downtown Denver, the wife of one Bronco player approached me after she had heard the news that Terrell had decided to write his autobiography

"Isn't it," she said, the distaste in her voice obvious, "a little early for that?"

To be truthful, it was neither unfair nor uncommon for someone to ask whether Terrell, at the age of 25, had experienced enough life to fill a book. Before this project kicked off, I have to admit that I wondered the same thing myself. But after watching and listening to Terrell spend hundreds and hundreds of hours reexamining his past, revealing his history, and reviewing every sentence of the book you now hold in your hands, I no longer wonder whether it is appropriate for a 25-year-old to share his life in words. I wonder why he didn't do it sooner.

Terrell doesn't have any children, doesn't have anyone wondering, "Where's Daddy?" but he still has plenty of dependents. His mother and the five children she is raising, most of his five brothers, many of his friends, and some of his former coaches turn to Terrell when they need help. When one of Terrell's childhood friends called him a couple of years ago and explained he had just wrecked his car and had to spend the money he had been saving for his wedding on car repairs, Terrell said no problem. He FedEx'd his friend a check for a few thousand dollars, enough to cover the costs of the wedding.

When Terrell's mom wanted a house big enough for her and the five children she is now raising, Terrell bought her one—in his development right up the street, not much more than 100 yards away from his house. When those five children—aged four to nine—need ski lessons or tennis instruction or ballet school or anything at all, Terrell is there for them, always there for them.

Terrell has been, and continues to be, his family's safety net; the person who is there to catch the people close to him if they should fall. He is his family's last line of defense. How many 25-year-olds could say that or play the role so willingly?

And even with all the adversity he has faced, he has maintained a perspective that few people his age—or really any age—have had. Last April, I showed up at Terrell's door a little over an hour before the 11:25 A.M. flight we were scheduled to take to San Diego, where he was to throw out the first pitch at the Padres home opener. Rang his doorbell, but no one answered. Called his cell phone, but no one picked up. Paged him, but no one responded. Frantic, with a good 30-minute ride to the airport still before us, I called the Broncos' training facility, to see if they happened to know where Terrell was. Sure enough, they did. Terrell was out on the practice field, running.

"Well, could you please tell him to run home—we have a flight to catch!" I said.

For whatever reason, Terrell had mistakenly thought our flight was at 12:20, not 11:20. Ten minutes later, he came speeding up his driveway. He ran into his house and grabbed his bags and we were off, racing to the airport. By the time we got there, it was 11:10—15 minutes before our flight. We ran inside the terminal, me telling Terrell we're dead, we're never going to make it. The woman at the check-in counter, who refused to give us our boarding passes because we were too late, told us the same thing. Our luggage would have to go on the next flight, and so would we.

Without another word about how we were going to miss our flight, Terrell raised his hands as if to silence us doubters and announced, "Keep hope alive."

With at least his hopes alive, we were off again, this time running straight to the gate. In maybe his most impressive run of the year, he led the way. Not only did we make the flight—maybe two seconds, tops, before the gate closed—but in San Diego our bags were the first ones off. And when Terrell saw our bags heading toward us, he grinned like he never had a worry, like he knew something all along.

"See. What'd I tell you? A one-in-a-million shot is a what? . . . A shot."

How often does a person get dragged into the San Diego Padres clubhouse so that a future Hall of Fame outfielder, Tony Gwynn—who has won eight batting titles, more than any other player in baseball history other than Ty Cobb—can ask for his autograph? That happened to Terrell last April. A month earlier, Green Bay Packers running back Dorsey Levens went out of his way to greet him with a handshake, an embrace, and the words, "Terrell Davis—the superstar himself!"

The beauty of it is that none of this kind of admiration has affected Terrell in any great way. He still is the same old Terrell, still thinks of himself as normal as you or me, even if his life is hardly as normal as yours or mine. Terrell relates to people, and people relate to Terrell. This, I believe, is because Terrell developed as a person before he developed as a player, and he developed as a player before he developed as a star.

Just last winter, when Terrell was dining out in Los Angeles after taping a guest appearance on the TV sitcom *Sister, Sister,* some guy noticed him and came right over to congratulate him on the Broncos' big Super Bowl win. The two hadn't been talking for more than a minute or so when the guy asked Terrell why he wasn't wearing a Super Bowl XXXII MVP jacket or something that advertised that there was a big-timer in the house.

"Come on," he told Terrell, "you gotta flaunt that!"

"Man," Terrell said, waving off the man, "that's not even me."

That tells you something, maybe everything, you need to know about Terrell. He is as humble as a backup, as real as his memoirs, not any different from what he was the day he showed up in Denver as a sixth-string running back. When it comes to people, he is a "TD"—in the truest sense of the expression.

Before we set out to do his memoirs, I asked Terrell why he wanted to do a book. "I think my life appeals to underdogs, people who don't think they can do something but actually can," Terrell said. "I just think it can inspire people."

And after hearing him tell his story, after hearing about all the guns and murders and alcohol and drugs that sucked in some of his family and friends but failed to suck him in, I honestly believe you will agree. It is a story that, if not read from the beginning, would be hard to believe in the end. And in the end, the sum of any book is entirely how it leaves you feeling. I think that when you close the covers of this book, you will not care or even notice that Terrell Davis is 25 years old.

In a hotel room just outside Denver, moments after he had finished talking to about 200 Colorado physicians about migraine headaches, Terrell eyed three 8-by-10 glossy color prints that had just been dropped in front of him.

Each one was some type of head shot of a smiling Terrell. The first was of Terrell performing his patented Mile High Salute. The next was a standard head shot, the kind you would see in a high school yearbook. And the third was of Terrell flexing, his biceps Popeyeing out of his arms.

"Would you mind signing a little message, something simple, on each?" asked Harry Rhome, a consultant for Novartis, the pharmaceutical company that makes Migranal nasal spray and employs Terrell as its spokesman.

Rhome was hoping to pass out copies of the autographed pictures in each city where Terrell was scheduled to talk about how much Migranal had helped him during Denver's Super Bowl XXXII win over Green Bay.

"Not at all," Terrell said. "That's cool."

Terrell picked up a black felt marker, stared for a moment at the first picture—the one of him doing the Mile High Salute—and scribbled, "I salute you.—Terrell Davis."

He then picked up the second picture—the one of him smiling and posing in a standard head shot—looked it over briefly, and scribbled, "Be at your best every time.—Terrell Davis." He carefully blew on the ink, making sure it was dry so it wouldn't smudge, and placed the second autographed picture on top of the first.

Then Terrell picked up the final picture, the one of him flexing. He glanced at it for a moment, lifted the marker, and scribbled, "You have the strength to overcome any obstacle.— Terrell Davis."

Most celebrities and athletes are famous not only for who they are but for keeping their distance. They don't ever let you get close enough to touch them. But after being allowed to get closer to Terrell than just about any other person these last few months, after being with him early mornings in Las Vegas and late nights in Los Angeles and full days in New York and San Diego and Denver, after getting to know him the way you know your best friends, I am convinced that it is all different with Terrell Davis.

You don't have to touch him. He touches you.

—*Adam Schefter*
May 13, 1998

1

OUT OF SIGHT

The gun ending the first quarter of Super Bowl XXXII had just gone off. It felt like it got me right between the eyes. Right then, my vision went. Just like that. And I knew that not only was the start of the second quarter now moments away, but so was a migraine headache.

As I found my way back to the our sideline, my only thought was, "Oh, no, this is not happening, this is definitely not happening!"

I could see nothing clearly, not the colorful Super Bowl XXXII banners hanging all around San Diego's Qualcomm Stadium, not the Bronco trainers trying to fend off my migraine, not my teammates asking me if I was all right, not the Packers players, for whom I was supposed to be causing headaches. An estimated 800 million people spread across 188 countries could see it all clearly, yet all I saw was a kaleidoscope of pain.

You want to know what I was seeing, exactly? The things you would be seeing if you crossed your eyes.

Try it, painful as it might be.

Not pretty, is it?

"I can't see!" I announced near our sideline to anyone who would listen.

"What's that?" our head coach Mike Shanahan said as he wandered over to me, not wanting to believe what he was hearing.

"I can't see!"

"Okay," Mike said as he placed his right hand on my left shoulder, as if everything was going to be just fine. "Just do this. You don't worry about seeing on this play because we're going to fake it to you on '15 Lead.' But if you're not in there, they won't believe we're going to throw the ball, okay?"

Now, I love my coach. The man is disciplined, structured, organized, detailed—he was the main reason we were in this Super Bowl spotlight to begin with. But how could he honestly think I could play when I couldn't see anything?

Well, I hadn't questioned him before, from the moment he drafted me out of the University of Georgia in the sixth round of the 1995 draft to the moment he gave me a starting job during my rookie season to the moment when I became a Pro Bowl running back. And I wasn't about to start questioning him now.

Like the good No Limit Soldier and team guy that I am, I glanced up at the scoreboard I couldn't see, ran back onto the field, somehow found my way back to the huddle, and strapped on my helmet. The play—"Fake 15, Lead QB, Keep Pass Right, Fullback Slide"—was called. The ball snapped. I took a fake handoff from Elway, and ran right toward the line and into the teeth of the Packer defense and linebacker Bernardo Harris. While the Packers were running at me—and I only know this because I've seen the replays at least 40 times since then—John was quarterback-sneaking into the end zone. Touchdown. Just like coach predicted . . .

While all I could see was one weird blotchy collage, I could definitely hear the 68,912 people at Qualcomm Stadium turning the place into a noise factory. Great—but my head didn't enjoy it, not one bit. I managed to spot Elway and give him the Mile High Salute. But now, with the play done and the left side of my head pulsating and throbbing, I needed help right away. Back on the our bench, I found it.

I was treated like an emergency-room patient, all kinds of immediate attention. Bronco trainer Steve "Greek" Antonopulos ripped open his medicine bag and grabbed the dihydroergotamine nasal spray—these days, better known as Migranal—that he keeps around just for me. It's what we use to abort my migraines, which usually hit about 30 or 45 minutes after my loss of vision. Without wasting a moment, Greek stuck the spray right up my nose. I took two sniffs in my left nostril, two sniffs in my right nostril.

And threw up.

Just super.

It had all started on an innocent enough play, "18 Hand-off," when I ran outside and cut back inside. For some reason, Packer defensive tackle Santana Dotson thought he was playing kickball, not football, and the guy leg-whipped me, and leg-whipped me real good. I pinballed into Packer safety Eugene Robinson, then crashed into the ground. Now, I don't want to make it sound like I'm blaming those guys, because I'm definitely not. All they'd done was trigger something I had actually set up.

A little confession here, time to come clean. I haven't told anyone until now, because I was just too ashamed of it. But I'd fumbled before I even stepped on the Qualcomm Stadium field that day. I'd forgotten to take my preventive migraine medicine, Indocin, which I consider my own little MVP—Most Valuable Preventer.

Usually I take my Indocin about one hour before any practice or game. Just pop the pill, swallow, and I'm good to go, don't have to worry about any migraine headaches hitting that day. Ever since I started taking it, I hadn't experienced a single migraine during any of our games.

The last time I had a migraine was the 1996 regular season, when we played San Diego at Mile High Stadium in Denver on October 6. At that time I hadn't yet started taking Indocin. Since then I had gotten braces on my teeth, given up coffee, stopped eating Big Macs, started seeing a chiropractor and neurologist, begun taking Indocin, and done everything possible to make sure I never would have to see cross-eyed in a football game again. It had worked.

But now, instead of a football helmet, I was wearing an oxygen mask, helpless. Instead of taking handoff after handoff, I was taking deep breath after deep breath. And all the while, I was talking to The Man Upstairs.

"Please," I was begging The Man, "let there be light."

This migraine was something I had been preparing for ever since the 1996 season, when I suffered two migraines four games apart: the first against Tampa Bay, the second against San Diego. As I sat on the bench during both of those games, I had kept asking myself, "What if this ever happened to you in a Super Bowl?"

My whole concern was not for the games against the Buccaneers and the Chargers, but for a future one, for a bigger one. For this. In both of those regular-season games, I fortunately defeated the migraine—and the team defeated our opponent. Against Tampa Bay, I came back from a second-quarter migraine and had 15 second-half carries for 94 yards during our 27–23 win. Against San Diego, I came back from a second-quarter migraine and had 11 second-half carries for 45 yards during our 28–17 win.

And after those wins, I told myself: "See, T.D., that's what would happen if you ever got a migraine in the Super Bowl. You'd fight through it the way you've had to fight through things your whole life."

That's just the way it has worked with me. Some players have always dreamed about playing in a Super Bowl. Me, I worried about playing in a Super Bowl with a migraine.

Now it was happening. And I was responsible for it, not the Packers or any of the hits they'd put on me. With all the hoopla of the Super Bowl, with all the excitement, I'd just gotten wrapped up in it. I'd gone through my normal pre-game routine, making sure my ankles were taped, helmet adjusted, shoulder pads tightened, socks pulled up to equal height, Nikes tied nice and tight, and a visit to the bathroom to do all my personal business. It's my own little checklist, the same for every game. Once I go through it, I know I'm good to go.

But right before I ran out onto the field, as I was sitting at my locker about 10 minutes before kickoff, I realized what I had forgotten from my checklist. I threw the Indocin in my mouth, swallowed as fast as humanly possible, but my mind was messed up. I was freakin', man.

Panic, that's all I can say—panic. It felt like I had overslept and was late for the game. Before I was introduced to the crowd during pre-game, I was not enjoying the moment the way I should have. While other players were running into the stadium, looking at how packed it was, seeing the array of colors everywhere, watching the fly-by planes and the fireworks filling the sky, totally taking in this moment most players never get to experience, I was thinking, "I took my pill too close to kickoff! I'm done!" And at the end of the first quarter, once I took the hit from Santana and Eugene, I was. On came a raging, head-rattlin', mind-blowin' migraine.

My punishment for being so stupid and irresponsible on the biggest day of my life.

At first I blacked out, couldn't see a thing. A few seconds later, I recovered some of my vision and enough of my senses to get to my knees. But I could not get up, not exactly a good thing for a running back who is supposed to be carrying the ball and a lot of his team's and city's Super Bowl hopes. And the next thing I knew, Greek was making like some kind of Olympic sprinter, dashing onto the field and right up to my side.

"Don't get up and try to walk," Greek told me. "Just stay there."

So I did as I was told, stayed right there, not moving. Which NBC had to love, even if my team didn't. I mean, they were getting $1.3 million for each 30-second commercial during the Super Bowl. All I was getting were words of encouragement.

"Just relax," our tight end Shannon Sharpe said.

"We need you back," John Elway told me.

And I knew they did. Believe me, the last thing I wanted to do was let down my teammates, the organization, my family, all the fans back in Denver. I've waited all these years for a team to depend on me the way the Broncos have, which is so unlike anything I went through at Long Beach State University and then Georgia, where I transferred for the start of my sophomore season. Through high school and college, I used to look at other running backs and wonder, "Why don't I get the ball 20 or 25 times a game?" But no one looked at me to make any plays. Now it's different. Now the Broncos look for me to make plays. And I wanted to get back up, get back in the game, help the team that depended on me.

After about two minutes, I managed to get up and walk to the sideline. My equilibrium was back. I could walk straight. I felt stable—stable enough so that I went in for another play, the final play of the first quarter. It was a two-yard carry to the Packer one-yard line.

Then the gun went off.

The first quarter and my eyesight were gone.

After Elway's touchdown run, after I found my way back to our sideline, I sat on the end of the bench, a white towel draped over my head, an oxygen mask with a green cord strapped to my face, throw-up caked to my feet. From all the clamor, one voice emerged. It was Mike Shanahan's.

"Just take him into the locker room," he told Greek.

Now, as unpleasant as it was to hear Mike ask me to go back into the game at the onset of my vision loss, this made up for it. The idea of getting away from the noise in the stadium and relaxing in a peaceful and quiet locker room was as sweet as a touchdown run. I knew that some R and R, combined with the Migranal, would clear up my head a whole lot quicker than sitting on any bench.

The training room had to be the quietest place in Qualcomm. I closed my eyes, wiped down my face. The only noises I could hear were the ones in the distance, the P.A. announcer calling out all the first downs Green Bay was starting to rack up before the end of the first half. Packer first down at the 32, Packer first down at the 21, Packers first down at the 11. To me, it sounded like there was no stopping Green Bay quarterback Brett Favre and the rest of his teammates.

Right after the Packers went the distance and scored a touchdown—making the halftime score Denver 17, Green Bay 14—I could hear my teammates marching into the locker room, their cleats clack-clack-clacking on the concrete ramp. One player yelled, "We gotta do something!" Oddly, the shout did not bother me. I opened my eyes, realizing the Migranal was starting to take hold. My vision was gradually returning. Objects were coming into focus. From the training room, I could actually read the nameplate on my locker, TERRELL DAVIS 30, as well as the nameplate on the locker right next to mine, HOWARD GRIFFITH 29. I could see my clothes, and Howard's clothes, and our shoes on the floor. I was feeling like I had been touched by The Man's magic wand.

Across the room, I could make out our second-half plan of attack, the 10 plays that our offensive line coach Alex Gibbs had diagrammed on the chalkboard. "19 Toss, H–2 Pass, 18 Handoff," on and on, all 10 plays I now believed I was going to be okay to run. Not only could I see our plays, but I also could see which of my teammates was saying what to me.

"Man, we really need you," our offensive tackle Tony Jones told me. "I know your headaches are back, but you can have those headaches tomorrow. We've got a Super Bowl to win here."

I was feeling revived and relieved. I could see, hear, do anything without any problems. The Migranal had worked. It had slammed down the migraine, tackling it before it could tackle me. As a test, to see if I was as right as I thought I was, I pulled aside Dr. Ziporin, a team physician, and asked him to throw me a football. Dr. Ziporin flung me passes, testing my vision like he was some kind of cross between John Elway and Dr. Green from *E.R.*

Dr. Ziporin didn't throw anything like John, but then, he didn't need to. I caught a few passes, and could see enough of the football to know I was back. Everything looked sharper, the colors looked brighter. I couldn't remember ever seeing things this clearly before.

You know how people say, "Just give me a second chance and I'll do it even better." That's how I was feeling. As the halftime entertainment show died down and the field cleared and the teams started to gather in the tunnel leading out to the field, I was living a second chance. And there was no way I was going to waste it.

As I ran back onto the field, my dream was in motion.

2

TAKING THE FIFTH

Well, well," our left guard Mark Schlereth said as we hud-
dled up right before the first play of the second half.
"Look who it is, guys. Hey, T.D., glad you could join us."

Hey, me too. My migraine was like the 17–14 first half
we already had played—history, man. I was seeing crystal
clear now, and I wanted everyone in the huddle to know I
wouldn't be leaving them again anytime soon.

"Sorry I was gone for a while there," I told everybody.
"But I'm cool now."

I was excited about being back. And I was even more
excited that on the first play of the second half, with a first-
and–10 on our 23-yard line, Coach Shanahan called my
number. The play—"19 Toss"—was a little sweep to the left
side of the field. I wanted the ball again. It showed that the
Broncos had confidence in me. But I didn't reward them
for it.

As I took the pitchout from John Elway, I felt like I had
a little spunk in my step. I turned upfield, ready to gain

some yards, when all these bodies converged on me, started grabbing at me. I was trying to pull free and break loose of the tackles, maybe a little too hard, when all of a sudden I felt the football and our lead slip right out of my hands.

The football went through my legs, and I tried to put them together and squeeze as hard as I could. But Packer cornerback Tyrone Williams reached between my legs and pulled the ball out. I was thinking, "Damn! This can't be happening!"

Packers ball, first-and–10 at the Bronco 26-yard line? Packers ball, first-and–10 at the Bronco 26-yard line. One headache after another.

"Sorry about that, man," I told Shannon as we walked to our sideline.

On the sideline, I told our wide receiver Rod Smith, "That won't happen again."

The Packers turned my mistake into a 27-yard field goal and a 17–17 tie game. But I turned it into a form of motivation, telling myself this is the chance you always wanted, make the most of it. And I'd like to think I did. From then on, I just kind of vibed the rest of the afternoon.

Normally I talk to myself throughout the entire game, but this day I did it even more than I ever had. Before each play, I was like, "Okay, Terrell, here we go, here we go!" For some reason, that just got me going. The ball would be snapped, I would be getting ready to take it, and I would be telling myself, "You've got to be ready, you've got to be sharp, you've got to be strong, you've got to run hard!"

Bottom line? I was out there realizing this situation didn't come around too often. And I also was realizing a running back might have a bigger impact on the game than any other position. The way I figure it, if a running back gets the ball 20-something times a game, what he does with it will change the outcome of the game. And this was the

Super Bowl! So I was, like, "Geez, if I can just hold on to the ball and start making some big plays, we can win this thing."

From the time we beat the Kansas City Chiefs in the American Football Conference Divisional Playoffs to the time Mike Shanahan showed us the "When We Were Kings" video the night before the big game, I felt great about our chances in the Super Bowl. But let me tell you the exact moment when I knew we were going to win the game.

When John Elway made like a helicopter and took to the air.

On a third-and-six play from the Packers 12-yard line, with about 1:20 left in the third quarter and the score tied at 17, John took off around the right end and instead of running it out of bounds, he turned it upfield. Packer safety LeRoy Butler was there to greet him, and when John saw him, he used his self-described "three-inch vertical leap." John jumped, and lifted himself and the whole team. By the time he spun around in midair like a helicopter and landed with eight yards and one of the biggest first downs in Bronco history, our team was going crazy.

John got up and threw his hands up, and I was, like, "Yeah, man, it's on!" I could feel this certain type of energy racing through our team. Anyone out there on the field, or even watching the game, could feel it.

You know how people say that certain players lead by example? When we saw John jump in the air without any regard for his 37-year-old body, we realized if he was doing that, we couldn't do anything less. You think it's accidental that two plays later, I ran one yard up the middle for my second touchdown of the game and a 24–17 lead? I might have gotten the score, but John and our offensive line got the assist.

From then on, the second half just flowed for us. Every time we ran the ball, we were getting big chunks of yardage. It felt like we were just systematically marching down the field, like clockwork, all business. Same was true on our game-winning touchdown drive, in which I gained 21 of our 49 yards, and I was seeing better than ever. The holes I was running through were wider than the Midtown Tunnel.

Which is kind of funny because the Tuesday night before the game, I was out with my agent, Neil Schwartz, and another one of his clients, Packer defensive end Darius Holland. We were at the House of Blues, hanging out, when Wyclef Jean of the Fugees pulled me up on to the stage and had me start singing "Guantanamera." That was the fun part of the night. The not-so-fun part came when Darius kept sticking his big, meaty forearms into my chest.

"What the hell you doing, man?" I kept asking him every time he did it.

"I want you to get used to how it's going to be on Sunday."

Well, put it this way. Darius's prediction was about as bad as my singing. With the game and a place in history on the line, we drove from the Packer 49-yard line to the one-yard line. One yard from the happiest day of our lives, Mike called for the "Fox 3 Run," a delayed handoff we hadn't run in a goal-line situation all year. Around the goal line, you usually don't want to delay anything, you want to attack. But, after watching hours and hours of game film of Green Bay, Mike had spotted a weakness in the Packer defense. And now he thought he had the perfect play for exploiting it. As it turned out, he did.

With 1:47 left in the game, I took the handoff and went up the middle, into the end zone, without Darius or any other Packer laying a forearm, or even a finger, on me. In fact, strangely enough, the only person who got beat up on the play was Packer coach Mike Holmgren. He was the one who had instructed his defense to let us score so that Green

Bay would be able to get the ball back with enough time to score.

Me, this is the way I figure it. We were going to score regardless, no doubt. But as a player I never would want my coach to tell me and my teammates to back down. That's sending the wrong message. You're telling your team, "You can't stop this guy anyway." You're quitting, and that goes against my nature. And in the NFL, one yard is a long ways. With three downs, we could have had a botched snap or a fumble or a penalty or who knows what. Then what happens?

Just look at our game during the 1996 season against the Chicago Bears. With 40 seconds left in a game that we led 17–12, the Bears had a first-and-goal on our one-yard line. It would have been really easy for Coach Shanahan to let them score and hope we would get the ball back with enough time to score on our own. But he didn't. He told our defense to dig in, to give up nothing. And that's what happened. On four straight plays—two runs and two passes—the Bears didn't gain a yard or the touchdown. We won the game.

And I saw the same thing happen in college. We were playing Auburn and they had a goal-to-go on the one and couldn't get in for the win. I've seen crazier things happen than a memorable goal-line stand. But Green Bay's Coach Holmgren made his let-them-score decision, and I'm happy he did.

The Packers did get the ball back in time to run seven plays, but they did not advance past our 31-yard line. And when Packer quarterback Brett Favre threw a fourth-and-six pass to tight end Mark Chmura that Denver linebacker John Mobley batted away with 28 seconds left, the Broncos—losers of their first four Super Bowl games—had taken the fifth! Bedlam and the Broncos ruled!

Even though my mind didn't comprehend the Super

Bowl win, it felt like something huge had just happened. There were so many people on the field, so much smoke from the fireworks, I couldn't see any of my teammates. But then I felt someone grab me.

"T.D.!" John Elway shouted, hugging me.

"I'm so happy for you," I told him, hugging him back. "Now, tell me you're coming back next year." You know, always thinking ahead.

John and I were supposed to get together, look into the cameras and announce, "We're going to Disneyland!" But we got separated in the crunch of people, we couldn't find each other again, and we never got to shoot the commercial. Remember Rocky, when he's in the boxing ring and he's calling out Adrienne's name and he can't get to her? That's how this scene felt. "Hey John, John, J-o-h-n . . ." Not only could I not find John, I couldn't even find some daylight to get back to the locker room to celebrate with my teammates. A damn golf cart had to take me back there later, I was getting so mobbed.

In the midst of the commotion, I heard an announcement over the P.A. system say that for my 157 yards and Super Bowl–record three rushing touchdowns, I had been selected as Super Bowl XXXII's MVP. Me? It was hard enough to believe I was playing in the Super Bowl in my hometown. But to win it? And to win the MVP? I'll be honest, winning the MVP—just as Marcus Allen, who went to the same San Diego high school as me, had done the last time an American Football Conference team won the Super Bowl—didn't stick out the way somebody might think it would, not then. All that mattered to me at that point was winning the Super Bowl.

During the ride back to our team hotel, the Hyatt in La Jolla, I reflected on the game, how huge it was. It was everything I had expected and more. It was big plays and lasting images. It was like no other game. With a whole mess of thoughts, I was, like, "We won the Super Bowl!" And, "We won the game, but damn, we almost lost!" And, "How lucky am I that the Packers had been able to convert my fumble into only a field goal rather than a touchdown?!" And, "How stupid that was to forget to take my Indocin?!"

I was thinking how wild this whole thing was. And I was realizing this was how things worked in life. You're going to be dealt some crazy hands sometimes; The Man's going to give you some cards that you really can't work with, but you've got to try to persevere. You've got to keep on pushing, man, just keep on pushing. No matter how many times you get knocked down, on or off the football field, you've got to get back up.

After the game, someone told me that the NBC analyst Joe Gibbs wondered on the air what I could have done if I hadn't missed the second quarter. Like, maybe I could have run for more yards than any running back in Super Bowl history. Me, I don't live in the world of ifs, ands, and buts. I'm a results-type person. We won the game; that's all that matters.

Sure it would have been cool to rush for over 200 yards to set a Super Bowl record, but at least I didn't have to live with the guilt I might have had if I had missed more time and we had lost the game. Forgetting to take my Indocin is something that could have cost us the game, the glory, and the world's championship. Fortunately, it didn't. And now that we've won, and the Vince Lombardi Trophy is in the trophy showcase at the Bronco training facility in Englewood, Colorado, I can let the truth slip out the way my fumble did without anyone getting mad.

By the time we arrived at the hotel, I was too drained to enjoy any of the all-night festivities. All I wanted was some quiet time with my family and a patented T.D. power nap. I mean, I don't know if people realize how long that Super

Bowl was. That seemed like the longest game I'd ever played in my life. The migraine was long, the halftime was long, the quarters were long, the TV timeouts were long, it was all so long and stretched out by the time we got done that I was totally wiped.

And I wasn't done with my work until I had taped two TV segments back at the hotel, one with ESPN, the other with the NBC affiliate in Denver, KUSA. Then, finally, I was free to go straight to my room, 726, to marinate. Upstairs, I ate a chicken sandwich, some french fries and greeted my family as they all arrived in my room. There was my mom, Kateree, and her daughter Jackie, and my brother Reggie and his wife, LaShonda, all kinds of people. As I lay on my bed, we talked all about the game, what they saw and what I saw, one big verbal replay.

Finally, after a couple of hours they left, and I was alone in room 726. Now, I don't know this for sure, but I'm thinking there aren't too many Super Bowl MVPs who have celebrated their big day with their family, a chicken sandwich, some french fries, and an early night in bed. I'm thinking most MVPs and Super Bowl winners keep the party going all night.

But it just goes back to me being an ordinary guy and me getting my rest. I get my rest, I'm happy.

The next morning, I had more reason to be happy. I got a ride in the backseat of a San Diego police car, this one voluntary. Last time I was in a spot like that was my freshman year of college, when the police were taking me away for trying to steal parts of a car. Now, as Super Bowl MVP, they were taking me away to give me my own new car.

The police escort took me to the San Diego Convention Center for the Most Valuable Player trophy presentation. The NFL commissioner, Paul Tagliabue, was there telling reporters, "A great, great, great performance, a great young man." A Ford Motor Company spokesman was there, presenting me with my choice of a blue F-Series Super Duty pickup or an aqua-blue convertible Mustang GT. Wild, man.

"So, Terrell," the Ford Motor Company guy said, like he was some kind of game-show host or something, "which will it be?"

The Mustang. It was for my brother Reggie, who—along with lots of others—was at my side that morning. So I'm guessing everyone went home happy that day. Reggie, who lives in San Diego, had a new car and Ford didn't have to worry about shipping it very far. Now the Mustang sits in the garage of the San Diego house we grew up on Latimer Street, along with a whole lot of memories.

I still think about the Super Bowl all the time. I'll be sitting at home, right in the middle of a video game, and I'll just break out in this huge grin and say, "Man, we won the Super Bowl!" Throughout my house I have all kinds of Super Bowl paraphernalia, hats and shirts and videos and pictures. And reminders of the Super Bowl seem to pop up at the strangest times.

Last April, when I was flying to San Diego to throw out the first pitch at Qualcomm Stadium for the Padres home opener, I was watching a *Seinfeld* rerun on the airplane's video monitor. Right after *Seinfeld* ended, a special NBC sports program came on. And I couldn't believe what it was. They began showing the replay of our game-winning Super Bowl XXXII drive, with Dick Enberg doing the play-by-play as he actually had done that day.

My eyes widened. I sat up in my seat. I was taking it all in, every play. Watching our team made me feel like I was back at Qualcomm all over again. There I was, with two minutes left in the game, running from the eight-yard line to the one-yard line. There were the officials calling our tight end Shannon Sharpe for a holding penalty that moved us back to the 18. There I was, with 1:47 left, cutting through three defenders and going 17 yards, back to the one.

Now, I sat on the edge of my seat, waiting to see the touchdown that sparked a controversy in Green Bay and a celebration in Colorado. But just as John was about to hand me the ball, the screen went blank. And a voice came over the P.A. system: "This concludes the audio and video portion of this flight . . ."

What?! I jumped up in my seat, higher than John did on his big third-down scramble. Man, I was hot! I wanted to relive those moments, my most memorable moments! But it just wasn't happening. United did something the Green Bay Packers could not do that day. They shut me down.

I didn't get to watch the ending.

My father didn't either.

3

POPS

My father, whom I like to call Pops, had a favorite expression. He used to tell us all the time, "I brought you into this world, I'll take you out."

As if to prove it, one night when I was eight, maybe nine years old, Pops had a little too much to drink and, about two A.M., came stumbling into the bedroom I was sharing with three of my brothers. Mom and Pops were separated, and Pops was living with us, the four youngest boys—me, Terry, Bobby, Reggie—in a little house on Florence Street in San Diego. On this night, Pops must have been really drunk.

He pulled each of us out of bed, lined us up against the wall, pulled out his .38 special with black electrical tape around the grip, and just started shooting. Right in our direction.

There were four shots in all. I'm, like, "What the hell?" He wasn't shooting at our heads, but right above them. Putting holes in the bedroom wall.

Not one of us jumped or moved or ran under the bed to hide and start crying. We knew Pops wasn't going to kill us, not his four youngest boys. We knew Pops was a good shot—an excellent shot—and if he wanted to take us out, he easily could have. All he was doing was toughening us up, making it so that nothing would ever scare us.

When it came to living with Pops, my brothers and I saw guns so often it became as routine as seeing the ice cream truck. One night in November 1981, right about the time Pops fired off his .38 special over our heads, I tucked myself into bed, fell asleep, and then, next thing you know, at about two in the morning, I woke up again. With a gun being pointed at my head. This time, it was a policeman's gun.

While this cop aimed his gun at my brain, others stormed the house. They pulled me and my brothers out into the cold night in our underwear, lining us up against the garage. I didn't know what the hell was happening.

Later on I found out that Pops and one of his buddies were in the house drinking and getting high, and they got into a confrontation. Pops's friend went home, came back with a shotgun, and just started firing away at our house. So in self-defense, Pops grabbed his gun and started shooting back. All of a sudden, our little neighborhood in southeast San Diego was like the O.K. Corral. These guys were having a shootout in our front yard.

As usual, Pops won. That was our Pops, all right. He nailed his friend in the arm or leg, some spot not too bad. The friend didn't die, but the police came and took Pops away. Again. They charged him with unlawfully owning and possessing a gun, but I think it wasn't even Pops's fault. Even in some legal document filed with the Superior Court for the County of San Diego, Pops's representation wrote that "the victim was the initiator, willing participant, aggressor, or provoker of the incident" and that Pops shot the guy "because of unusual circumstances, such as great provocation, which is unlikely to recur."

This was the world that our family became really accustomed to, the way it was growing up a lot of the time.

Around our house, Joe Earl Davis—Pops—called the shots.

Pops was from Missouri, and he let anyone he was about to fight know it. "I'm from the Show-Me State," he would say, challenging them to be as tough as their talk.

Partly because of his confrontational style, Pops wasn't always around to raise me and my brothers. He was imprisoned in St. Louis in 1963 and 1966 for robbery, and then again in San Diego in 1975 for grand theft, and 1981 for having that shootout. Don't know exactly how many years he served in prison, other than that it was quite a few. But when Pops was around, he taught us things most boys don't learn. Mainly how to be tough. When I was younger and my mom would try to spoil me, Pops would get pissed.

"Don't baby him, don't do that!" he would yell at her.

If she would introduce me by saying, "This is the baby," he would yell, "He's not the baby! He's the youngest! He's not the damn baby!"

Pops was that kind of guy, and if you wanted to be in his family you had to be tough. I still remember how he would slap me, smack me, grab me, punch me, and, most painful of all, stab me in the chest with his index finger. That hurt as much as anything, but it all was to toughen us up, to get us ready for our own battles.

Pops believed we were going to have to be fighters to make it. He showed us how to load guns if we ever were threatened and needed to use one. He showed us how to use the pocketknives he gave us to take to school if anyone challenged us to a fight, and it was a good thing he did.

When Mom and Pops were separated, in 1980 and '81,

we lived with Pops over at his house on 3763 Florence, just off Thirty-eighth Street and right up the street from St. Jude, the school I went to from kindergarten through sixth grade. Basically, we were the only black people in a predominantly Hispanic neighborhood. Sometimes when my brothers and I walked to school we would find ourselves in these little rumbles. Actually, a lot of times we would find ourselves in rumbles. The neighborhood versus the Davis kids.

I remember one time I ran home to tell Pops about a fight, and Pops whupped me something good because I'd left my brothers behind to take on about nine other kids. I was only trying to help, to get Pops to the scene, but it didn't matter to him. To Pops, the only way to help our family was to stick up for one another. We had to defend our name and our family. If one of us got into a fight, we all had to fight, regardless. That was the way it had to be.

Pops exposed us to a lot more than a typical kid would normally see. Around our house, I would find little doobies and little buds of marijuana leafs that Pops would be smoking often. I never actually saw him deal drugs, but I'm guessing he did—he kept a little scale around the house to measure out the amounts of marijuana he would stuff into plastic bags. I might have been young, but I wasn't naïve.

Pops did a lot of drinking. One of my aunts used to call him Black Velvet, after his drink of choice. Looking back, I guess I see that Pops was an alcoholic. That was all he used to do, drink. Not like it was any great secret around town. People would see Pops walking down the street, bumping into things, stumbling his whole way home from the welding job he had over at A–1 Welding on Imperial Avenue.

I saw plenty of women around the house when Mom and Pops were separated for about a year and a half in 1980 and '81. Pops would bring home his lady friends and sit around with them on the couch, kissing, smoking, drinking, fooling around. It was just another thing Pops tried to expose us to, sex.

I would also notice a lot of goodies around our house that would just show up out of nowhere. Stereos, TVs, alarm clocks. One of my older brothers once said Pops would take some things every now and then to help out the family, but I never knew too much about any of that. All I know is that when we needed something, Pops made damn sure we had it.

Pops never tried to hide his lifestyle. I don't know how other people feel about it, but I honestly thought, for me, it was a good way to grow up. Being exposed to so much meant that when we encountered things in the outside world, outside our house, nothing could shock us. And nothing did. When my friends were smoking weed or drinking scotch or having sex, I wasn't in any kind of rush to join in. The novelty of it already had been taken out. The curiosity factor was gone. All because of Pops.

But even with the crazy life he led, Pops was still a disciplinarian. He didn't play around too much. You messed up, Joe Davis was there to put you in your place. And boy, would he ever! When we got in trouble, whuppings were the norm for us—me, Joe, James, Reggie, Bobby, and Terry—and, every now and then, even my mom. So I didn't mess around, I didn't get into a lot of trouble because I knew if I did, Pops would beat the hell out of me.

When Pops beat us, he would make my brothers and me strip down butt-naked and whip us with an extension cord. Mom would plead with him to let us at least put on underwear to soften the blows, while I would be thinking, "I hate him, I hate his guts!" I didn't say it to his face, I wouldn't ever tell him that. But as the cord snapped against our skin and as the welts instantly began to form on our arms and back and booty, all I could think was: "I hate this man! I wish he'd go away! I wish he'd just die!"

These were some serious lashings. One time when I got sent home from school with a migraine, I was delirious, out of my mind. I remember walking in the front door and trying, unsuccessfully, to hang my coat in the closet. My motor skills were shot, useless. Hard as I tried to hang the coat, I just couldn't do it. And Pops got mad, real mad. He ripped his belt out of his pants, screamed at me to pull down my pants. As I struggled to undo my belt and zipper, his voice was like a knife in my head. The pain he inflicted on me was even worse. Pops whupped me something bad.

Much as I hated it, I didn't too much care when he hit me or my brothers. I cared a lot more when he hit Mom. I hated the fact that he used to hit my mother. During the time when they were separated, without realizing the consequences, I once told Pops that Mom had a new boyfriend. He got real pissed off about that, and he roughed up my mother pretty good, with all the kids watching. What he did to her made me cry, it bothered me so much.

Pops may have done some things that you might frown upon, but he always provided for his kids, he always looked out for us, he always protected us. There was always food on our table, there was always a bed to sleep on, there was always a roof over our heads. He was a complicated man, and believe it or not, he was the most loving father I ever could have wanted.

Mom used to work in nursing homes and she saw plenty of patients come in with virtually no family history in their files. It's like the family is one big unknown. That's the way it is with Pops.

I do know that Pops's mother, Rose Davis, left the family in St. Louis and moved to somewhere in Arkansas where she died in 1973. Pops's father, A. C. Davis, fought in World War II, though no one seems to know exactly where. When A. C. Davis returned to the United States, he lived in

St. Louis until he died in early 1998. Pops's brother, Larry, lives in St. Louis, but the last few times Mom has been there and tried to get in touch with him, she has had no luck. And Pops's two sisters, whose name no one in my family seems to know, live somewhere in Arkansas. So there's Pops's family tree—barren, without leaves.

From what I understand through my relatives, Pops's family was pretty dysfunctional. I've heard that Pops's mom drank and his father sometimes neglected him, and it just wasn't a really good overall situation. The stories I've heard about them are some of the same types of things I used to see happen with Pops, when he used to drink or get into trouble. So I'm guessing Pops's behavior was just consistent with his family's.

Still, Pops showed us love, lots of love. Just when you thought this man was cold, he would throw you off. He would come home from work with candy, toys, all kinds of goodies. He would give us money to go out and party. He would buy us bikes, skateboards. He would bring us home the cutest German shepherd puppies you ever saw. He would spoil us in that ways few fathers spoiled their kids.

And Pops was funny, and I mean hysterically funny. I'm telling you, the man was funny enough to be on Comedy Central if he wanted. We would sit there and just laugh at the way he would act for hours. He would blast some Al Green or the Temptations or the Four Tops records, and would grab my mom and his boys, and we would just start dancing all around the house, everywhere. At the family picnics, he would have everyone cracking up during all the card and dominos games. And when he was drunk, he was really funny. We would drive around with him in his car, and a lot of times, we almost lost our lives with this man. He would be swerving all over, running people off the road. People would tell us they'd seen Pops driving down the street and that he'd almost hit a man. That was just him.

Usually, though, he wasn't driving. Pops loved to walk. He was notorious for it. I don't mean like walking up the street, I mean like walking miles and miles. If we wanted to go downtown, we would walk there. Downtown was a few miles away, at least, and it seemed even farther when you were a little kid. But we would walk, and as we walked, Pops would let us stop at all these shops to eat french fries and ice cream, to buy tennis shoes and T-shirts.

He would walk to all of our Pop Warner games, too. Even though he had six boys, it seemed like Pops was at every one of our football and baseball games, cheering us on louder than any other father there. A lot of kids didn't have their parents at the games, but we always could count on Pops being there.

Someone once asked my oldest brother, James, his feelings about Pops and the way he raised his boys. He feels the same way I do, the way everyone in our family does. Without Joe Davis around, no doubt some of the Davis boys would be dead, like so many of the other kids in our neighborhood who grew up without any fatherly influence.

Pops was the one who shaped and molded me, more than any person I know. Pops made me the person I am. I still see a lot more of Pops's personality in some of my brothers than in me, but I guess I've got some of Pops in me, too. I know Mom thinks so. She says that I look just like him. And she thinks the similarities are even more obvious on game days. When she's at my games watching me run, she can't help thinking that I act and move just like Pops did.

April 17, 1987, sticks out in my mind more than January 25, 1998, the day we won the Super Bowl. It was about one year after Pops had been diagnosed with lupus, an immune-deficiency disease in which the body doesn't recognize itself and it starts to attack itself. On that April day, when I was 14 years old, my three youngest brothers and I were playing baseball on a little dirt field at Valencia Elementary School. In the middle of our game, Dorothy Woodland, a longtime family friend, showed up and told us that our mom wanted us to go to the hospital.

We got into her car and drove off with her. The previous week he had been admitted to Mercy Hospital. Dorothy was awfully quiet, and I started getting a bad vibe. Pops had been sicker than I could remember and he hadn't looked well. He hadn't even had enough strength to open a can of soda, and one day our neighbors called to tell us Pops had fallen down outside the house and couldn't get up. We thought he was drunk, but it was really that his body was deteriorating so quickly he could barely stand.

It didn't help matters that Pops, stubborn guy that he was, refused to take his prednisone, the medication he was supposed to be taking daily. His whole attitude was "screw my medicine." He would only take the prescribed pain reliever, but that wasn't enough.

At the hospital, things were quiet. We took the elevator up to Pops's floor and got off. Just as we turned the corner, we saw Mom coming toward us. She was trying to be calm, but she couldn't be. She broke down. And my whole stomach dropped. Mom didn't have to tell me or my brothers anything. I didn't believe it, didn't want to believe it. But we knew.

I still remember my brother Bobby, who was 16 years old at the time, dropping his head and crying, "NO! NO!" . . . I still remember my mom crying, and feeling how much it hurt me to see her so hurt . . . I still remember me and my three brothers slowly walking into Pops's hospital room, staring at the strongest and toughest man we had ever known now lying in a hospital bed, hoping he would blink, hoping he would move, hoping he would get up, hoping the doctors had misdiagnosed him. But there was no hope anymore, only tears. My brothers and I just grabbed Pops and hugged him one last time.

Pops died on Good Friday, the seventeenth of April. Six days later, on his forty-second birthday, he was buried at Greenwood Cemetery in San Diego. When he died, I thought about it a lot and I felt guilty—and I still feel guilty—that I was out playing baseball while he was passing on. I could at least have been at the hospital with him, saying good-bye. Then I realized the thoughts I used to have when I was younger, when he was beating us, and I was like, "Can't believe I used to wish that upon him." Once Pops was gone, the only thing I wished then was that he'd be right back there with us.

For the next three weeks after his death, I just sat in my room, going through different stages. At first, for about a week, I was in disbelief and denial. Then I accepted it and spent the next week mourning. And then, by the third week, I was trying to recover from it. More than 11 years later, I still haven't. I don't think I ever will.

I think about Pops a lot now, a real lot. I think about how when I have kids, hopefully before I'm 30, I'm going to make sure they're as tough and disciplined as Pops made us. There's going to be a lot of Joe in me, no doubt. I'm not saying I'm going to whup them, but, whenever they do come along, I'm going to discipline my kids good, teach them right from wrong and love them.

Pops's presence is definitely missed, in a whole lot of ways. My mother is raising three foster children, plus two grandchildren. We always look at it now and say, "Man, if Pops was here today, Mom's five youngest kids would not be acting as unruly as they do." Mom's doing a great job raising them, but still, that discipline element is missing. Pops would keep them in check, just like he did with us.

And you know, if Pops were here, I really don't think he would be as hard as he was back in those days. By now, I think he would have mellowed out. Seeing the eight grandchildren he would have today, which he always wanted real bad, would have melted the man. Now he would have them. I wish he were here to see it, man, so much I can't even tell you.

I went to visit Pops a couple of times at Greenwood Cemetery, but it was just too painful, so I stopped. But there are still reminders of him all the time. Anytime I see other players with their fathers, it reminds me of my own. When I was driving to Mile High Stadium last November for our Monday night game against the Oakland Raiders, I was thinking, "What if Pops were here?" When we were at the Super Bowl, with all the headlines and attention and parties, I kept thinking, "Man, what would Pops think of all this?"

And I always wonder, if he were here, what he would think of me? Hopefully he's up there looking down at me, and hopefully he's proud of me the way I'm proud of him. Mom says if Pops saw what was going on with me now, he would be ecstatic, she could not even imagine what his expression would be. She says he would not believe it, and I don't think he would. I mean, I don't. The boy he tried to toughen up has toughed it out all the way to the NFL.

4

MOM

"Mom," I always tell Kateree Lawanda Davis, the woman who brought me into this world and is still the most important woman in my life, "you have to say no. Please. Just learn to say the word 'no.'"

"Yeah, baby, I will, I will," Mom assures me.

But she still hasn't learned, not after all these years, and she might never. When we were younger and living in San Diego, she never said no to anyone. Anyone who needed a good meal or a place to sleep or any of life's basic necessities was welcome in the Davis home on Latimer Street, no questions asked. She was—and is—so willing to give of herself to people and never feels put upon. She is the most loving and generous person I know.

Mom took in my best friend Jamaul Pennington in 1989, when his mother met up with some hard times; my friend Michael Doolittle in 1986, when he didn't know where his next meal was coming from; and my grandfather

Nishel Thomas in 1984, after he had a stroke and became bedridden. She never said no to any of them.

And it wasn't like it was just those three, that was hardly it. Our front door was one big revolving door, kids coming and going all the time. I would say that at various points of my childhood, Mom had at least 20 different people outside the Davis family of eight living with us on Latimer, in the five-bedroom, two-bathroom house. One time I can distinctly remember having 12 people living under our roof. It wasn't like we were the Rockefellers, but still, Mom found a way.

And when we got older, when the family spread from San Diego to San Francisco to Denver, nothing changed even then. Things got even crazier. When my brother Terry and his girlfriend at the time had a baby girl, whom they named Lawanda, in 1988, they turned to my mother for help. They figured Lawanda would have a better life with Mom, so Mom took in her granddaughter.

In 1991, Mom became a foster parent to two more infants: Jackie, whom the San Diego foster-care agency placed with her, and Tyree, whom my brother Terry had fathered. A year later, after Tyree was reunited with his own mother, it was almost like Mom had an opening and she took in another baby boy named Kayle, who also was placed with her through the foster-care agency.

Those were all the new additions my mom's new family was supposed to have—Lawanda, Jackie, and Kayle. But in 1993, my oldest brother, Joe, and his girlfriend had had a baby boy named John Jr.; in 1996 the girlfriend abandoned John Jr. and his older sister, Jalessa (who had a different father), and my mother took on both the children. Mom went through the process, filled out the paperwork, officially became their legal guardian.

So now, my mother—who turns 50 in December and should be kicking back at her new home near me with her six sons taking care of her—is all busy taking care of five more children: Lawanda, 9; Jackie, 7; Jalessa, 7; Kayle, 5; and John Jr., 4. It's one thing to take on kids who are normal kids, problem-free kids, but these kids have faced some serious adversity.

Mom has been told that four of the five children's natural mothers had problems during their pregnancies. Now the kids and my mom, all living under the same roof, fight through this together.

The toughest battle belongs to Jackie, who was born two months premature, weighing just over two pounds. Later, she was diagnosed with ADD, attention deficit disorder.

To help control her, Mom felt she had no choice but to put her on the drug Ritalin, something that enables Jackie to focus, on stay on task. Mom fears that Jackie might have to be on this drug her whole life. It pained my mom to put her on it, and even when she talks about it now, tears well up in her eyes. But the drug seems to be working. Jackie has been able to prosper in school and participate in group therapy and not have any more problems.

An amazing person, my mom. Mom figures if she turns away these kids, where are they going to go then? So she doesn't ever stop being the type of person who takes on responsibility. If you don't have a place to stay, if you don't have food to eat, if you don't have the necessary things to live, my mom will provide that for you. I have so much respect for her. She's my hero, she's definitely my hero.

Up until Mom was six years old, while my grandmother was establishing a career as a nurse, she lived in St. Louis with her grandparents, Nishel and Alta Thomas. Nishel Thomas was a butcher at the Swift Packing House and Alta Thomas was a night office cleaner.

Her grandparents were the biggest influence in her life until she was 16—at which time she met my father, Joe

Davis. On the last Sunday in August 1964, Mom was washing dishes at home when one of her friends, Joanne Guy, stopped over with news about a party on the west side of St. Louis.

She left with Joanne, and when they arrived at the party, Mom, the way I've heard the story, noticed Joe Davis right away. She didn't waste any time. She walked right up to him, introduced herself, and asked him to dance, not wanting nor willing to hear an answer anything close to no. Joe and my mom danced, and didn't stop until eight months later, when they were married in April 1965. Mom was 16, Pops was 19.

Mom's mom apparently was not really happy about the marriage. She was not crazy about the fact that Pops was working a blue-collar job in a paper factory, he had been in and out juvenile halls growing up, he had just spent a little time in jail for getting mixed up in some type of robbery, and when he and Mom decided to get married, Mom was pregnant with my oldest brother, Joe. Mom felt that once she left home to marry Pops, returning home was not an option.

Her grandparents also were disappointed and hurt that Mom got pregnant, got married, did the type of things they didn't approve of. Mom and Pops were not welcome to live with them, either. Ultimately, Mom and Pops decided to live with Pops's father, A. C. Davis, for two months. Then they did the only thing they thought they could. They got their own apartment and tried to settle into a life that never seemed, from what I can gather, very settled.

Mom had her first child, Joe, in August 1965. When Mom was pregnant with her second son, James, Pops got mixed up in another robbery and went to jail, in July 1966. Mom was 17 and should have been graduating from Beaumont High School in St. Louis. Instead she had one baby at home, another on the way, and no money. With no one else to turn to she moved in with one of her girlfriends. The she began to make an income—not a really big one, but something—after December 1966, her eighteenth birthday, when she went to work as a spare-parts inspector at McDonnell Douglas, an aircraft plant.

It was a lonely and hard life. She needed help, and fortunately, a kind and quiet man 12 years older than her, a concrete-liner maker, was there to give it to her. While Pops was serving about three years in jail, this guy and my mom struck up a relationship that made her life a little easier and happier, and produced her third boy, Reggie. The year Reggie was born, 1969, also was the year Pops ended up getting out of jail. He and my mom got back together, and led the typical life of any poor young couple. They paid their rent, had their parties, played some cards, drank some beer, and kept wondering if things would ever get better.

Meanwhile, they produced two more boys, Robert in 1970 and Terry in 1971. And as they began to raise five boys, two of my parents' friends—one man named Charlie, the other called "Po' Boy"—were shot and killed during robberies in St. Louis. It was at that time, with five boys already under their roof and with little old me on the way, that Mom decided she could not live that life any longer. It was time to leave St. Louis.

Her grandfather Nishel Thomas and grandmother Alta Thomas, the people who had helped raise her, had moved to San Diego in 1968. Her grandfather had been writing her letters on an almost weekly basis, telling her about San Diego's sunshine and palm trees and better life. The letters gave Mom all the pointers she needed about where she should move her family.

So in September 1972, one month before I was born, Mom washed and ironed our family's clothes, packed them up in a trunk, and bought $100 worth of bus tickets for her and her five boys to get the heck out of St. Louis. Pops stayed behind because he still had his job as a kitchen-cabinet laborer. And a day and a half after the bus pulled out of the Greyhound station in St. Louis, the Davis family— minus Pops—arrived in the sunshine and palm trees and what were supposed to mean the better life of San Diego.

That's my mom, an independent and strong woman. To move out at age 23, to a place where she didn't know any-body but her grandparents, where she didn't have a job, where she didn't have anything, that says a lot about a per-son. What she went through in San Diego, and the way she carried herself out there, says even more.

Pops joined the rest of the family out in San Diego in October 1972, right before I was born. Six months after my birth, Mom went to work as a nurse's aide, making $300 a month. Then she started taking basic college classes at San Diego City College.

Right about this time, Pops went to prison for about six months for reckless driving. While he was in jail, Mom was accepted into the Licensed Vocational Nurse program at City College. And that same year, with $600 down, Mom bought the family's first house, at 3763 Florence.

Those days were really crazy for Mom. She would be up long before five A.M. fixing fried chicken dinners for the family, waking up her boys and fixing them Cream-of-Wheat breakfasts, then dropping us off at school so she could get to her nursing classes by eight. After school, she would pick us up, fix us dinner, work double shifts for four dollars an hour at local hospitals, and come home and start the same old long days over again.

Pops got out of prison in September 1976. Like every couple, Mom and Pops went through some good times and bad times. The good was in 1979, when we bought the new five-bedroom, two-bathroom house on Latimer, where my brother Reggie and his wife LaShonda still live today.

While they were building the place back in 1979, our family used to go over and take pictures of the house every day, as if we couldn't believe we were going to be living in a place so much nicer than any we had lived in before.

But things weren't too good during Mom and Pops's separation in 1980-81. Mom took her two oldest boys, Joe and James, to live with her on Latimer, and the four youngest brothers, including me, stayed to live with Pops on Florence. On weekends, though, all the boys would always wind up staying with Mom. Her place was a drop-kick away from Martin Luther King Park, which was where we had our Pop Warner football games.

Not only would we stay there, but it seemed like every-one else in the neighborhood would, too. Everyone loved my mom, and she became kind of like the team mom: hav-ing kids over all the time, letting everybody sleep over when they wanted, cooking everyone all kinds of great food. Oh, man, can she cook! She used to make egg rolls and fried chicken and baked pasta, and she had this one thing called shepherd's pie—with ground beef at the bot-tom, mashed potatoes and corn in the middle, and cheese on top—that tasted like nothing else I've ever had.

Only thing better? When Mom and Pops got back together for good. We were one big family again. But it didn't last as long as Mom, or any of us, would have liked. Lupus killed Pops six years later, in 1987. Among a whole bunch of other things, it meant Mom would have more responsibilities than ever. She had to be Mom and Pops.

Not easy for Mom. She took care of us all and never said boo about it. Knowing how tough that was on her, I did what I could to help. I tried not to give her any trouble, to take care of her as much as possible.

When she asked me to take out the garbage or clean my room, I didn't fuss with her, I did it. When she was at work, and I got home from school early, I would try to wash the dishes and clean the house and mow the lawn and make sure she wouldn't have to do any tidying up once she got home from work. I even cleaned up the messes that my brothers' girlfriends used to make when they lived with us. It was important for me to do that. I figured, why should Mom come home from work, only to find more work waiting?

I wanted to give back to her for everything she was giving to me, which was plenty. I was her baby and Mom treated me like it, spoiling me. I remember one time I told her I wanted to buy this white scooter so bad, and Mom was always, like, "Okay, we'll find a way to get it," and we always would. Another time there was this skateboard I felt like I just had to have, and Mom found a way to get that for me. And in college, it was Mom who helped me make the $200 monthly payments on this '87 gray Chevy Blazer I was driving around. Whenever I needed money for anything, she would do whatever it took, even if she had to scrape and fight to get it.

She was always there for me, always. When I would come home from school sick with a migraine, she would leave work and come home and take care of me. When I went to Georgia, and didn't realize the weather would get as cold as it was, Mom mailed me big care packages of thermal tops and bottoms, hot cocoa and soup, all kinds of goodies to help me at a time when she couldn't be there.

For all the times she was there, and is still there, I am indebted. I try to show her how much I appreciate her and love her whenever I can. During my second year in the NFL, when I heard that her car kept breaking down, and how upset she and her five children were getting, I told Mom I would buy her a new minivan. She was so excited because she went out, test-drove some cars, called me back, and told me she had found the one. We arranged for her to get it and the day she did, she couldn't stop calling me, she was loving it that much.

"Thank you, thank you," she told me, all excited. "It's great. Already got eight hundred miles on it."

That felt great. To have my mother calling me and telling me how she's loving her vehicle and how she's driving it around everywhere and how she can't believe how happy she is? It felt good to reciprocate.

In August 1997, she packed up her five children and all their belongings in that very same van and headed out of the city she had called home for just about 25 years, to Denver, to my home.

Now, I had started hearing some rumblings the previous spring that my mom was thinking about changing venues, about wiping her slate clean and starting a new chapter in Denver. My aunt, Karen Livingston, told me about it first. Then I heard it from one of the family friends. Then another friend, and another. Then one day my mom called me up to discuss her future.

"What do you think about me moving to Denver," she said.

"You're not moving to Denver," I said.

"Yes, I am. I'm moving in August."

And that was it. I just think Mom was tired of the same old San Diego scene, a lot of people coming and not going, those same people taking advantage of her big heart, kindness, and hospitality. She probably thought the rest of the family in San Diego all had each other, while I had barely any family in Denver. She probably figured, "Let's start things over, enjoy a different life."

The immature side of me didn't want my mother moving to Denver. I thought, "I'm in the NFL, I want some room, I want to be able to go places in the city and do what I want to do without having my mom around overseeing the whole experiment." But then the mature side of me said, "You know, after eight years of living apart, it would be real cool to have my mother come out, to have her enjoy some of the time I'm having in the league. Because it's not going to last forever."

So I was ready for her. I wish I could tell you I was ready for her five kids. When they pulled up to my home and they all jumped out of the van and ran into the house, reality set in. I was, like, "They're here, and they're here for a while." For one month, in my house, I had six new roommates.

Oh, man, it was crazy. The kids were sliding across the hardwood floors, running up and down the stairs, pumping up the volume on the TV cartoons, screaming at almost all times. And this was at seven in the morning! Every morning! They were the last ones to go to sleep at night and the first ones up in the morning, and let me tell you, they took over my house. I lost all sense of peace and quiet. Every once in a while I would get home from practice and no one would be in the house, and I'd be, like, "Oh, they're gone!" And I'd throw myself on the couch for one of my patented power naps.

Next thing you know, before I could doze off, I'd hear, "BEEP! AUGH! AAAY!" My peaceful respite would be over. The kids would be home.

I think my mom felt kind of bad because here I am trying to prepare for upcoming games, get ready for my job, and all around me, there are all kinds of distractions. She knew something had to change, so she started looking for an apartment and found one about 15 minutes north of where I live, right by Lowry Air Force Base. By September, she and her kids were out.

It was not like we stopped seeing each other. Mom would have a hot meal waiting for me every Sunday night when I got home from my game, some fried chicken or lasagna or something good and tasty. Other nights I would drive over to her house and hang out at her apartment and talk to her about all the things that were going on. And when I wasn't home, she would come to my house and feed the fish and bring in my mail and just make sure that my house didn't burn down and it was still functioning when I got back.

All the while, she was carving out a little life for herself and her family in Denver. In the early winter, Mom got a job as a teacher's assistant at Whiteman Elementary School in Denver, grading papers, monitoring the playground, running copies, things like that. She began making more and more friends, particularly in my neighborhood when she would come over and watch my house while I was in Kansas City or Oakland or some other NFL city. And she even started looking for a new home.

She started looking way out north and worked her way farther and farther south, closer and closer to where I lived. Finally, the home that she found and loved was in the same housing development I lived in. Right up the street. Not much more than 100 yards away. She told me she had zeroed in on a home in my neighborhood and asked me how I felt about that. I was, like, "In my neighborhood? Ma . . ."

Knowing that she could not get to her house without passing my house first, I figured she would be stopping over at all hours, checking up on me. At first I thought, "Nah, this is not a good thing." But then I thought about it again, more and more, and I was, like, "Yeah, yeah, that's a great idea." Mom would be close, she would be in the same neighborhood, I would get to race cars or shoot baskets with her kids, and I've always envisioned having my whole family living nearby.

So I was, like, "Mom, won't you be my neighbor?" That was an offer she never would have said no to. We arranged for her to move into the house in August, right about the time I would be getting home from training camp. My new neighbor, my mom.

Mom is going to be the President of the Terrell Davis Salute the Kids Foundation, as well as a board member for the Terrell Davis Migraine Foundation. We're going to be like the Boys Club, and give all kinds of kids all kinds of opportunities they might not ordinarily get. We're going to arrange for them to have home tutors and personal computers and athletic equipment, things like that. And you tell me, who better to run it than my mom? Who knows kids any better?

Mom's also getting more and more involved with the Mothers of Professional Players Association, a concept she was approached about at the Pro Bowl last February by the mothers of the Baltimore Raven offensive tackle Jonathan Ogden and the Tennessee Oiler running back Eddie George. The organization will be like a support group to help players with difficult decisions and issues. For example, if you know of a certain agent who's no good, or a financial adviser who's a crook, it's your job to speak up. If a player is new to town, it's up to one of the mothers to take him in and feed him a home-cooked meal.

I don't know how she does it, how she has the drive to do it all. She wants to help me out; she wants to help the children out; she wants to help the community out. She has all these different incentives and motives for doing what she does. But I know one thing: You can't question that woman's heart.

Still, it's not an easy life, Mom's. It looks like it's getting better and better all the time, but the one thing I still would like to see added to her life is a companion, a husband. From the time my father passed away, I've never seen my mom with a date. It's sad to me that she doesn't have someone to grow old with, to take vacations with, to share life's experiences.

My mom could offer somebody the biggest heart and the warmest love, but she still thinks she comes with too much baggage. To a degree, it's true. Most people don't want to go out with somebody who has so many kids running around the house. But Mom is so into those kids. She gets her love from them.

In return, she gets it back from everyone. Everyone who knows her knows she deserves a Lifetime Mother Achievement Award for her Hall of Fame career. But she doesn't want any awards, any attention, she doesn't want anything except the knowledge that the children of this world are being looked after. Mom has sacrificed a lot to make sure that has happened, but in the end, I'm guessing it has been worth it. She's proud of the fact that she and her family have, after some struggles, finally made it.

People ask me all the time how I feel about being a role model. To me, role models are not athletes or entertainers. Role models are people you can look up to, people who do something constructive for society, even though they might not necessarily be on TV. The doctors, the teachers, the coaches, people like that. People who are helping other people, like my mom.

5

ALL FOR ONE AND ONE FOR ALL

Shut up and don't move!" the San Diego police officer yelled at me, slamming my face into the hood of his car. "You move an inch, your ass is his!" With that the cop motioned to a big old German shepherd whose face was so close to mine, I could smell his breath, feel it. The meanest-looking dog I ever saw was barking and breathing all over me, just waiting to get himself a little late-night snack. Now, growing up I once had a German shepherd that we called Bonnie. Let me tell you, I didn't remember Bonnie having a temper like this dog's. Even if I didn't move an inch, it seemed like my ass still might be his.

I didn't move again until they took me away. In hand-cuffs. I rode in the back of a San Diego police car, just like I did the morning after we won the Super Bowl. Difference was, instead of being escorted to the Super Bowl MVP award presentation to accept that new aqua-blue Ford Mustang, I was being whisked away to jail for trying to steal some new Dayton spoke rims.

I should say here that I'm no angel. People look at me like I've never done anything bad or stupid in my life, and I don't want to kill anybody's dreams and images, but I'm human, too. I've gotten into trouble like just about everybody else at some point when they were younger. It all comes down to choices, making the right ones. I didn't always do that growing up. The older I got, the more I started thinking about my future and the consequences, and the better choices I made.

But back on a weekend night during my freshman year at Long Beach State University, I made one of my poorest choices ever, one I'll never make again. One weekend I came back to San Diego with my girlfriend, Donna Sailor, and right about midnight on a Friday night, one of my childhood buddies called me up with an idea he thought I might like.

"Found this car with rims that'll fit your car," he told me. "They're sweet."

Now, those days, I had been cruising around town in my Chevy Impala—my rimless Chevy Impala. I'm thinking, you know, I could use some sweet new Dayton spoke rims.

"How long's it going take to get them?" I asked.

"Mmm, I'd say about thirty minutes."

"Cool."

Next thing I knew, we were off, driving to the scene of the crime. Only problem was, when we got there, we didn't have anything to jack up the car. So we drove around, found these plastic crates and tried them. But the car was just too damn heavy for them, and it all came crashing down. So we drove around the neighborhood once more, found some wood blocks, came back, and started jacking up the car again.

While my friend was stealing the rims, I was standing lookout, but neither one of us was doing a really effective job. In fact, we were doing some really sloppy work. I'm guessing we must have been there three, four hours trying to get those damn rims off. By the time we did, my friends' hands were filthy dirty and I didn't even notice all the policemen creeping up on us, ready to pounce when we tried to get away. But what did we know or care at that moment? We had ourselves four sweet new Dayton spoke rims for my Chevy Impala.

We took off from the scene, racing down the street, and not more than a few seconds later, police lights lit up the night. Lights came out of nowhere and everywhere. Police cruisers blocked us in. We couldn't move. One cop car was so close that, sitting in the passenger seat, I couldn't even open my door more than an inch. My friend opened his door and tried to run, but they caught him. And obviously, not being able to get out of the car, my running skills were of absolutely no use to me. They caught me, too.

"Hey, look, you got me," I told them, not even putting up a fight.

The police didn't care that I was all of a sudden in some kind of mood to cooperate. They weren't. They roughed me up pretty good. They yanked me out of the car, slammed me up against the hood of theirs, and the first thing I felt was the heat. The extreme heat of the car's hood. It felt like a furnace. And my face felt like it might melt right into it.

"Hey, this car is hot!" I yelled.

"Shut up and don't move!" one cop yelled. "You move an inch, your ass is his."

First the police took me to the San Diego city jail, then they slapped some shackles on me and transferred me over to South Bay Jail, a minimum-security prison in National City, about 10 miles south of San Diego. They charged me with grand theft because the value of the rims was over $500. I remember sitting in jail for four days, which seriously felt like four years.

I couldn't take it, man. I couldn't go anywhere, couldn't run around, couldn't talk to anybody, couldn't go to the bathroom without telling someone. But you know what? I'm thinking I had to see what it was like, because had I not gotten in trouble then, who knows? Maybe later on, when I was tempted to do some other stupid thing, I wouldn't have been as smart. And maybe I would have made another bad choice.

Of course, none of this made my mom feel any better at the time. Man, she was hot, hot, hot! She had to go out and hire a lawyer for me. The lawyer she brought to court told the judge I had no prior arrests, I had a clean record, I was in college, playing football, just trying to get by, could he please give me a break. The judge, buying into my lawyer's argument, obliged. He dropped my felony to a misdemeanor with a year's probation, and let me go back home with Mom.

And as I left jail, I couldn't stop thinking I would never, ever, EVER go back! Man, that is not the life for me.

Five more brothers, and we could have fielded our own 11-man offense. There's Joe, now 33, a plumber's apprentice in San Diego; James, 32, a teacher in San Francisco; Reggie, 30, an administrator at Qualcomm Inc., a software company in San Diego; Bobby, 27, who lives in San Diego but doesn't work; Terry, 26, a cook in Denver; and me, 25, the baby.

Joe and James were like the parents when Mom and Pops weren't around. They made sure we ate and had clothes to go to school, all that good stuff. They taught us how to put things together like our bikes. I remember Joe and I always used to make models of cars and boats and ships. Joe was real cool, but he was a lot older, so we didn't always play around. He was more of an instructor to me, telling me about the birds and bees, coaching me on some woman. Joe even showed me my first nudie book.

James was the more serious type. He did everything by the book, just as Pops had instructed him to. We used to have two nicknames for James: "Brainiac" and "Book Worm," because he was always the smartest one in the family, the one who spent the most time studying. He was always doing his homework, getting good grades, running the household. He came of age faster than most teenagers, and around our household, that helped out me and the rest of my brothers.

However, I didn't spend a lot of time with Joe and James, except on the weekends. When Mom and Pops separated, Joe and James lived with Mom. My three other brothers and I lived with Pops over on Florence Street. So growing up, the four youngest brothers were closest. Those were some of the greatest times of my life, hanging out with them. They were the best brothers I could ever have wanted, the kind of brothers who would always protect me and watch over me.

When we lived over on Florence, Reggie looked after us like he was Pops. Reggie was a stuntman. He used to ride bikes off walls, jump through the shower glass, do all kinds of crazy things. We used to call him Evel Knievel.

Bobby took on Pops's personality in every way. To this day, I still think Bobby was Pops's favorite son. Because Bobby didn't take anything from anybody, just like Pops wouldn't. He was a lovable, caring kid. For six years we slept in the same twin bed, and sometimes he would even let me have the whole bed to myself. He would just sleep on the floor.

Then there was Terry, who had to be my favorite, the brother I was most inseparable from. We were just a year apart and we had a lot in common. We played the same sports, liked the same things, so naturally I think we were the closest at that time. Terry and I played on the same Pop Warner football team, and when I say I was a Pop Warner legend, the "Boss Hogg" on offense, he was definitely the "Boss Hogg" on defense. Terry played cornerback and linebacker, ran back kicks and punts, dominated everything he did. Around town there was always a debate about who was better, me or my brother. To this day, people truly believe Terry was a better player than me.

I'm also lucky for another reason, besides having five great brothers who always looked after me. Being the youngest gave me the luxury of being able to look at them grow up, to study what was going on in their lives and then ask myself, "Do I want to do that?"

I got to watch Joe join the Marines and James join the Navy, which was really exciting to me at first. A long time ago, I had entertained the idea of enlisting and serving our country. But then I got to see how my two oldest brothers had to dress, how they had to act, how they had to live, and the idea faded from my mind real quick. For some people, the armed forces are the best thing. But I asked myself, "Did I want to do that?" and I was, like, "N-O-O-O!"

Next brother I studied was Reggie, whom I'm still really close with these days. While a senior in high school, Reggie impregnated one of his girlfriends. They decided to have the baby, a girl they named Kalina. I didn't think it was a bad thing, having Kalina, but I watched how it interrupted their high school days, how it disrupted their lives, how it affected them, how my Mom had to take care of the baby, how much pressure it put on her. And I asked myself, "Do I want to do that?"

Same as with my other brothers, I had the chance to learn from Terry, too. When he was in ninth grade at Bell Junior High School, on South Briarwood Road in San Diego, he was involved in this unfortunate incident that I know changed his whole life. One day he forgot to bring sugar to his cooking class and his teacher, an older lady whose name

I can't remember, got really mad and started making a scene, hollering at him like crazy. Terry didn't stand for it. He grabbed his teacher and threw her to the ground.

Even though Terry was only 14 years old at the time, assault charges were brought against him. The judge sentenced him to 240 days at Rancho Del Campo, a juvenile center in Campo, California, about 65 miles east of San Diego. After that, for a whole bunch of reasons, Terry never really got back on track. He missed school, he was always behind, he lost interest in football, he was removed from society way before he should have been, and to this day, as he's cooking pizzas at a Pizza Hut just outside Denver that's not too far from my house, Terry still talks about how much he regrets what he did. It changed everything in his life. I asked myself, "Do I want to do that?"

And then, there was Bobby. Besides me, Bobby is the only other Davis brother ever to make national headlines and land on the front page of the *Los Angeles Times* and *San Diego Union-Tribune*.

Even though he's not much bigger than me, Bobby was a hell of a fighter. He wouldn't just beat you up, he'd whup your ass. He'd whup people bad, to the point where they wanted to press charges. A few times Bobby came home and flipped out on the family. He would get so wild, we would have to call the police to come over and calm him down. And on the street he was doing some bad things, things that I would prefer not even to mention.

I'm guessing a lot of his temper and anger were hereditary, being that Bobby's makeup was identical to Pops's. We nicknamed Bobby "Sin"—as in "Sinister." With Bobby, we knew something not too good was coming. The only question was, when? When was on a March 1992 day, in an event that went on to become a front-page story in a whole bunch of newspapers, including the *L.A. Times* of October

23, 1993, under the headline NEW RIGHTS FOR FETUSES TOUCH OFF LEGAL DEBATE.

The nearly 2,000-word front-page story read, in part:

"Maria (Trinidad) Flores had just cashed her $378 welfare check when a stranger approached her and demanded money. Clutching her toddler in one arm, Flores defiantly refused to give up her cash. The man fired a bullet into her chest.

"She crumbled to the ground, rolling over and over in a vain attempt to grab the money. 'Dinero,' a witness heard her whimper. Her 20-month-old son hovered over his blood-soaked mother, screaming wildly.

"The early afternoon attack was like so many others in this run-down part of southeastern San Diego, and it probably would have been long forgotten by now if it were not for the fact that Flores was pregnant. She survived the shooting, but her not-yet-6-month-old male fetus was stillborn.

"The case has ignited a widespread legal debate— and a California Supreme Court review—over whether someone can be convicted of murder and face execution for killing a fetus so young that it could not live on its own and could be legally aborted . . .

"Robert Davis, an unemployed 19-year-old, was arrested. Prosecutors charged him with first degree murder of a fetus, potentially a capital offense because it was committed during a robbery. Davis also was charged with robbery and the attempted murder of Flores."

The story became huge, bigger than any the family had ever been involved in. The front page of all these newspapers, history-making stuff. Because of the heavy-duty abortion debate, everybody associated with the story became interested in the status of the fetus. All these abortion-rights and anti-abortion activists were speaking out everywhere about the situation, following it very closely, figuring the case could affect abortion rights in California and maybe even across the country. At one point there even was speculation it could affect the attempt to overturn the landmark *Roe vs. Wade* decision.

The front-page stories about the case kept coming and coming. It was written about in law textbooks. Then, in May 1994, the California Supreme Court ruled 6–1 that a person who kills a fetus that is at least seven weeks old can face murder charges and possibly the death sentence. But fortunately, the law was not retroactive to Bobby, meaning he was the last person in California who did not have to face the death sentence for shooting and killing a fetus. Bobby had become the person most responsible for the creation of some of the toughest fetal murder laws in the country.

Bobby still had to go to jail, and I was there, sitting in the courtroom, the day they sentenced him to life without parole. But on the basis of some technicalities in the case— basically that the fetus was not yet considered a person— Bobby no longer had to go to prison for life. He was served time in Folsom State Prison in Represa, California, from March 6, 1992, to August 13, 1993, and then was moved straight to the California State Prison in Los Angeles County in Lancaster, California. He was there until March 26, 1997, when he was paroled.

Man, the whole situation was really tough on me and everyone in my family, because here's your brother in the headlines for doing something terrible. The woman lost her child and our brother was going to prison and a lot of people's lives were affected. I felt bad for the woman, and still do. My brother paid for it, but this woman will live with the incident the rest of her life. Her child is gone forever.

Bobby can't run from that. It happened. Let it be known. Everybody—I don't care who it is—has their own secrets, their own skeletons in the closet. If people want to frown upon that, on the things that have happened in the past, fine, that's their right. But people change. I've changed, you've changed, my brother has changed. If you asked him whether he would do the same thing today—hell, no, he wouldn't, of course he wouldn't.

I'm thinking that people, especially kids, need to know that many of us aren't perfect, and that when we do get into trouble, we can change, and there can be better things ahead. If you get into trouble, don't look at the situation as the end of your life. Don't go on doing more crazy stuff because you feel like you're going off the deep end. Stop—you can turn it around. My brother is trying to turn it around right now, hard as it is. And I'm seeing that it's damn tough.

The problem with going to prison is that even though you might have been rehabilitated, when you get out, after spending all those years away, you're thrown back into society without a trade or skills. The first thing any prospective employer asks you is, "Have you been convicted of a felony?" That question is on every employment application, and you have to check yes. If you check yes, who the hell is going to hire you?

I know Bobby is sorry for what he did so long ago, but he can't go back and change it. Now he's trying to move on, but he will always have a dark cloud hanging over his head because of what he did back in March 1992. He can't go out and get a job, he can't go out and redo his life, and he's getting frustrated.

If I could, I would bring him to Denver to work in the Terrell Davis Salutes the Kids Foundation. But under the terms of his probation, Bobby cannot leave the city of San Diego. They're keeping this man in the city where he's had all these problems, where he's going to get caught up in the same cycle all over again. There are people in San Diego who remember what he did to them, who will seek him out, and who will want to fight him, stab him, shoot him, whatever.

So Bobby is just being put in a situation where he can't win, no matter how hard he tries. To me, it's just not fair. The court already has ruled he has served the necessary time, he's out of jail, and now, to me, he should be allowed to try to make a new life for himself. Mom has written a letter to his probation officer, practically begging them to let Bobby come to Denver, and after writing this book, I think I'm going to write one, too. Here in Denver we think we could help Bobby help himself.

But you know what amazes me, blows me away about the whole situation? When I think about it now, I think about the fact that none of my three oldest brothers—Joe, James, and Reggie—have ever gotten into any really serious trouble. Bobby and Terry didn't get to see the consequences of older brothers getting into trouble the way I did.

If the script had been flipped, and if I had been older than Terry and Bobby, who knows. Our situations might have been all reversed.

In February, I flew my brother James from San Francisco to San Diego, and my brother Terry and I flew from Denver to San Diego. So all the Davis brothers were in the same spot at the same time for a two-day reunion at the house we grew up in on Latimer, where Reggie lives with his family now. And man, it was emotional. It was the first time since our great-grandfather Nishel Thomas's funeral, on April 3, 1992, that we had all been together.

We were going to plan another reunion date, in another year or two. But we figured, we can't say we'll hook up then, we need to do it now. Ain't no guarantees about a year or two from now. There's never a promise that you'll be able to have six brothers together again, in the same spot at the same time. It reminds me of that expression some-body once told me. People make plans, and God laughs.

We're fortunate, man, because think about it. Statistically you have six black males from the same family in the 25-to-33 age group, all alive, all together. What are the chances of that? Probably not very good. Like so many of the people we grew up with—like Jamaul Pennington, who was shot and killed, and Michael Doolittle, who died of a drug over-dose—at least one of us brothers is supposed to be dead or in jail or involved in something not so good. But the Davises know something about beating the odds.

That first February night we were together back at the house was special. We talked about our expectations, our futures, our personal problems, Mom and Pops, and about how each of my brothers might be able to come work for my new foundation. We just sat around the table in the den, talking, laughing, telling stories late into the night.

We laughed about the time when all the brothers were seated at the dinner table and Mom said, "Joe, say grace," and he looked up and said, "Let's grub!" Mom slapped the hell out of him for that. And we laughed about the time Joe brought this big snake home from school and lost it in the house and it showed up a couple of days later in our oven, alive and slithering around. We laughed about the time when James and Reggie were little kids and they were playing in the car and they accidentally pushed the emer-gency brake, put the car in gear, and rolled backward into a brick wall.

Before we knew it, it was late, very late, about three in the morning. Looking around the table, seeing all the lives that had gone their own ways and had come back together for this one weekend gave me such a happy feeling. Usually when I went back home to San Diego, I would always see Reggie or Joe, but never James or Terry or Bobby. And when I was in Denver, I would see Terry, but not anybody else. Now everybody was there, the band of Davis brothers, and it was a perfect time for a toast.

I stood up and raised a toast.

"To being back together.... To all of us being back together."

6

HEAD GAMES

My head was pounding, pounding, pounding. Excruciating pain. And nobody—not my mom, not my dad, not me, not anybody—knew what in the world we should do. How could we? This was the first time I ever had a migraine headache. I was seven years old.

The pain was so bad, so miserable, I just kept thinking to myself, if this is what I have to go through, I don't want to live. Now, it never got to the point where I was raiding the medicine cabinet, or tying a noose, or holding a knife to my throat, or was on the brink of committing suicide. I didn't think like that, not as a seven-year-old, and not now. I just didn't want to live with the pain.

But you have to know exactly how I was feeling then. It's tough to describe—other than to say I was nauseated, I was vomiting, I was sensitive to light, to sound, to smell. To life. I wouldn't wish it on an Oakland Raider. What a migraine is, for the nonmedical people out there, is a neurological disorder that affects one side of your head. It's a lot easier to think about this way. It's like one big headache. One big headache times 50.

Doctors still don't know what causes a migraine headache. And when you're going through the pain, and when you have no idea what's wrong, it's even worse. My first one, I had just finished playing a Pop Warner football game for the Buccaneers, my first football team. I was in "4–5" park in San Diego, right on Forty-fifth Street, waiting in the parking lot for my mom to pick me up. As I waited, something made me look back at the field, at a light, and all of a sudden everything turned into patches of light. Everything. I lost my eyesight, started to panic, thought I was going blind. When Mom showed up about a half hour later, long after the other kids already had gone home, she found me slumped against a chain-link fence, crying.

"What's wrong?" she said.

"I can't see!" I cried, telling her the exact same thing I would tell our coach, Mike Shanahan, 18 years later in Super Bowl XXXII. "I can't see!"

By the time she got me home, about a three-mile ride back from the park, I could see. But now it was my head. I had a head-cracking-open-like-an-overripe-watermelon pain. Pounding, pounding, pounding. Mom gave me soup, tea, aspirin. None of it, unfortunately, worked. The only thing that helped was the crying. I went straight from the football game right to the crying game. That night, I cried myself to sleep.

When I woke up about midnight, I didn't feel too well and I threw up on my bedroom floor. Then I ran to the bathroom and tried to throw up some more. But I had nothing left. I leaned over the toilet, dry-heaving, throwing up my yellowed insides. I wiped my face with a towel, got into bed, and cried myself back to sleep.

When I woke up again, this time at about three in the morning, there was a dull roar inside my head, sort of like a hangover. The house was dark and quiet and lonely. Everyone was sleeping. My headache did feel, for the first time, a bit better. But I was really hungry. I went downstairs, fixed myself the biggest bowl of vanilla ice cream that you ever saw, and sat down in front of the TV. Couch potatoing even then.

After flipping through the channels, and finding there actually was more on TV in the wee hours of the morning than just static and national anthems, I found something that caught my attention—something that would have caught anybody's attention.

Naked ladies. Yup, right there in front of me, right on HBO, were a whole bunch of naked ladies. They were the first naked ladies my seven-year-old virgin eyes had ever seen. And they had parts—body parts, not acting parts— that I didn't know women had. I was loving it. HBO was showing the French movie *Emmanuelle* at a time when I was supposed to be sleeping, but wasn't. And I still remember the movie the way most kids remember *Willie Wonka and the Chocolate Factory*.

In the movie, a young French girl, Emmanuelle, has an older husband who encourages her to seek out new sexual adventures with men and women. The movie is still the highest-grossing French film of all time, and I understand why. Back then it was advertised as "X was never like this!" and even now, after all these years, I've got to agree.

As a little kid I sat there transfixed, staring at the TV and eating my big bowl of vanilla ice cream.

My first X-rated movie.

My first migraine headache.

All on the same night.

Migraines kept messing with my head all through junior high and high school. They would come every three weeks, and the only place I could find any solace and refuge was in dark, quiet, cool rooms. At Lincoln

High School, I actually played three full football games at nose guard with head-rattlin', mind-blowin' pain while I was trying to tackle running backs whom I could only see half of.

People tell me how brave it has been of me to play in these NFL games with classic migraines. Trust me. It's nothing compared to what I endured in high school and college.

The worst migraine I ever had, no question, came the summer before my senior year of high school. Our football team was in Washington, D.C., scrimmaging Cardozo High School, off Clifton and Thirteenth Street. We had just finished a practice and I remember walking to the buses, and there went my vision, just like that. Gone.

I told my coaches I had a headache, but they didn't have any idea how serious it was. They could not understand, just as I couldn't the first time I got one. They probably were thinking, "How can a little headache sidetrack a big football player?" So they forced me to go on our tour of the nation's capital, even though I would rather have sat in detention for a year straight.

One of the coaches told me to just sit in the back of the bus and be quiet. Quiet? How could I be anything but? I slumped down into my seat, rested my head against the window, and tried to relax, but I couldn't, no chance. All the kids on the bus were yelling and screaming, having a grand old time. My head was pulsating from the noise, from the movement of the bus, from kids accidentally bumping up against me. This went on for four hours, four miserable hours. They are four hours I cannot and will not ever forget.

Before the bus even left, I told the coach, "I don't want to go, I can't go, my head's killing me." His response: "These opportunities are rare," and he made me go see the

White House and the Lincoln Memorial and the Washington Monument, all the sites. I still remember him telling me, really clearly, that I might never be in Washington again.

Guess he wasn't banking on me making it back to Washington, D.C., to visit—and salute—President Clinton at the White House last June with the world-champion Denver Broncos.

But all the time I had these nasty headaches, my biggest worry was that no one had a name for them. Of course, it was not like people were willing to give me the same kind of medical attention I get today, when doctors treat each one of my headaches with the care that surgeons usually reserve for organ transplants. Back then, other than my family and friends, no one really cared who Terrell Davis was or how much pain I was in. I lived with my headaches the way some of my friends lived in poverty. No choice, man.

But football can change a lot of things for a lot of people, and it changed things for me. During a spring football practice at the University of Georgia, after I transferred there in 1992, I felt like I was right back at "4–5" park, playing for the Buccaneers. I had all the same miserable feelings. Blurred vision, uncontrollable nausea. It was hell before, and it was hell again. But the difference this time, 13 years after the first time I went through a headache times 50, was that I had some top trainers surrounding me.

One of them walked over to me, examined me, and told me, as if it had just been so obvious all along, "You have classic migraines."

I was like, "Yeah, Yeah. Migraines! I have classic migraines! That's exactly what I have!"

Strange as it sounds, I actually was excited to hear the news. It was like a revelation. Migraines. Migraines. It just sounded right, even though the inside of my head felt all wrong.

The good thing is that once you identify your problem, any problem, you can deal with it more effectively. Now, instead of the soup, tea, and aspirin Mom used to give me, I was prescribed Naprosyn, an anti-inflammatory drug that sure felt like it worked. I only had a few migraines the rest of my time at Georgia. One came while I was playing against South Carolina, and I sucked it up, just like I had in high school.

The Naprosyn controlled the migraines. But it didn't cure them. The migraines came right along with me to Denver. I had my first NFL migraine before my rookie season, at a minicamp about two months after the Broncos had selected me in the sixth round of the college draft. It happened at a June 1995 practice, and I knew exactly what it was right away. I told Mike Shanahan I needed some quiet time, away from the on-field drill work. I had pain on the brain.

Now that I know him, I'm sure I know what Coach must have been thinking: "A running back who can't play because of a headache? Great, just great. Some kind of tough guy we got here. No wonder he still was around in the sixth round of the draft."

The next time I got a migraine was during my rookie season, October. The Broncos' assistant trainer, Jim Keller, had to drive me home, as I was incapable of driving myself. Two more migraines came in the off-season after my rookie year, and then, for the first time in the NFL, during my second season, in September 1996, one came during a game. It was a nationally televised game against Tampa Bay.

I was on the field, and all of a sudden there was a bright light. I tried to see the ball, the defenders, the game that was going on all around me, but I couldn't. But I was prepared for this. Before the season started, while watching CNN's *Medical Report*, I saw a story about Lidocaine, a nasal spray that numbs the migraine before the migraine numbs you. I spoke to the Bronco trainer Steve Antonopulos about it, and we ordered some. This was the day we would finally see if the medicine was all that it was cracked up to be.

I stuck it up my right nostril, snorted, then stuck it up my left nostril, snorted. It was like a magic potion. Fifteen minutes after the migraine started, it ended. I actually went back into the game and carried the ball 22 times for 137 yards and one touchdown, and even though we had been trailing in the fourth quarter, we won 27–23.

So I had solved one problem. But I had created another. It seemed like everyone in the Rocky Mountains, and around the country, was watching the game. And everyone had a cure to suggest for my migraines. Calls were pouring into the Bronco training facility by the hundreds, maybe thousands. The switchboard was completely flooded. I remember the team's receptionist, Maeve Drake, telling one reporter, "These people are giving me a migraine, and I don't even get headaches!"

But that's how fans around Colorado are. Great fans, caring fans, just not all that educated about how migraines should be treated. One guy told me to find the spot on my head where it hurt, then find a really hard floor to rub my head on. Now what in the world is that supposed to do besides give my head static cling?

How about this one. Somebody told me I should inject myself with the urine of a pregnant horse. Now, I've got Bronco running thick through my blood, but I don't want any pregnant horse pee, or any horse pee, running through there too, you know what I mean?

Another guy suggested that I drive two hours to the top of a mountain and stand there, letting the fresh mountain air wash away the headaches. No problem finding mountains out here in Colorado, but sorry, sir. No way I'm doing that.

Everyone had an opinion. To me, the only ones that mattered belonged to the doctors, who told me that I needed to revise my diet by taking more magnesium and zinc. And while taking more of those, I had to take less of other things. They gave me all types of dietary restrictions. I listened, but here's a confession nobody knows. I don't follow all the rules.

If I took everybody's advice, I'd be messed up. I mean, c'mon, I've got to live a little, too. You're telling me no chocolate? No Coke? No Mickey-D's? No getting outside in the sunlight? I might as well live in a bubble, eating nothing but salad and water. No thanks. I can do without coffee, which I have completely cut out of my diet, but don't even think about taking away my Quarter Pounders with cheese.

I did make some lifestyle changes, though. For one thing, I began seeing a neurologist regularly. Her name is Dr. Judy Lane, and she works in Denver at the Rehabilitation Associates of Colorado. Smart lady, helpful lady. She's always trying to do anything she can to chase away these migraines. I spend more time with her during the season than the off-season, but she has been one of the most consistent women in my life.

I also got braces on my teeth in June 1997. Doctors believed the alignment of my teeth had something to do with the frequency of my migraines. And the braces— which I wore the whole time I was writing this book but which should be off by now, if I am a good boy and wear the rubber bands on them—are fine with me. I don't have a problem with them. To me, I'm trying to do what I can. And women, for some reason, love them, which I don't mind at all.

Some NFL players ask me about the braces, curious

about getting them for themselves. They don't want any-body to know, but they'll ask me about them before a game, and I've become the unofficial spokesperson for Wearing Braces. I give them a big-time endorsement, even though they do occasionally rip open my lip during foot-ball games and leave it feeling as raw as an open gash. That's just how it is. At first I used to come out of the game because I'd get my lip stuck in my braces. But eventually you form calluses, and after a while there's no problem.

But the people most curious about the braces? Kids. Kids are funny like that. They'll always say, "What's on your teeth, Terrell? Lemme see, lemme see!" And I open my mouth wide, flash them a smile, let 'em see. After see-ing them on an adult, they think braces are cool, and you know what? So do I.

All this, the medication and the neurologist and the diet and the braces, have helped me stave off my migraines. But from what I understand, we can only control migraines, we can never cure them. Looks like for now, as long as I remember to take the Indocin I forgot to take in the Super Bowl, we've got things under control.

The day after we won the Super Bowl, I went to Disney-land. Also got to do *The Tonight Show with Jay Leno*, one month after I had done the *Late Show with David Letterman*. I wasn't on Jay's show more than a couple of minutes when he started right in with me. Like a lot of people, he wanted to know all about my migraines, about how much of a problem they can cause at inopportune moments.

"Have you ever said to a woman, 'Not tonight, baby, I've got a headache?'" Jay asked.

Funny guy, Jay, but you know, he wasn't far from the truth. Back when I was going to Long Beach State, I took a woman I was dating named Donna Sailor bowling one night. We got to the bowling alley, I started hearing the plunking of pins, and the same type of blurriness started coming on. I knew just what was happening. So I told Donna, in so many words, "Not tonight. Got a headache." At least an oncoming one. And I left her at the bowling alley while I booked it out of there faster than any scout had ever timed me in the 40.

It was very ungentlemanly for me to leave her at the bowling alley, but she was cool with it, she understood. I had no other choice. I had to find a cool, dark room as soon as possible and avoid 24 to 72 hours of hell.

So these migraines can be good for a laugh, I guess, even though there's nothing funny about them to me or my family. My family still has concerns about my migraines, but because I know the history of them—when they come, how they long they last—I'm not too worried, I'm not scared anymore, especially now know that I know how to control them.

Now I'm trying to help other people with their fears. Right after the Super Bowl, I signed a deal to become the new spokesman for the Novartis Pharmaceutical Corp., and their Migranal nasal spray, which I used during the Super Bowl to prevent the full-blown onset of my migraine. Why not endorse the product? The stuff works fast, improves functionality, and lasts a long time.

It was funny because I found out the day after the Super Bowl that Chris Tama, the vice president of Novartis, was watching the game, watching what was happening to me, and thinking to himself, "I think we've just found our company a new spokesman." Forty-eight hours after the Super Bowl, Chris and my agent, Neil Schwartz, hammered out the deal, just like that. Since then, I've had a bunch of people ask me where to get Migranal, and I tell them it's available with a prescription in just about every drug store across the country.

I have a number of endorsement deals, but my deal with Novartis means more to me than any of the others.

Together, we set up the Terrell Davis Migraine Foundation, a program that was launched in April. It's going to educate a lot of kids about what migraines really are, and I can promise you that this foundation is going be really big in inner cities, I'm going to make sure of that. There aren't going to be any seven-year-olds up all night crying and throwing up the way I was, having no idea what was wrong with them. Now they will know.

And kids aren't the only ones who will be educated on the subject. Adults will, too. In fact, they already have, if my experiences tell me anything. With the help of my offensive line and the rest of my teammates and coaches, I was able to set a lot of marks last season. But the one that stands out to me is that now all people realize migraines don't have to be the debilitating illness that they have been all these years. You can revise your diet and see a neurologist and take Indocin, or Migranal, and you can fight your way through them. Just look at me.

In February, while I was in New York for the NBA All-Star game, a woman I had never met before walked up to me and thanked me, thanked me for being such a great example for her. All these years she had been getting nasty migraines at work. Each time she got them, she would call it a day, punch out, and head home. Now when she gets a migraine, she told me, she thinks about what I did in the Super Bowl. And she stays at work, determined not to let her migraines beat her the way they have for so many years in the past. Hearing that made me feel good, really good.

What would make me feel even better would be if they found a permanent cure for migraines. Then again, I know I've already found something that can help the 35 million migraine sufferers out there:

Vanilla ice cream and *Emmanuelle*. Did wonders for me.

7

"BOSS HOGG"

At Sharpe Hospital in San Diego, on October 28, 1972, Mom was exhausted and overjoyed. The moment after doctors ushered me into this world, they held me up so she saw me from the back. What Mom saw first was exactly what she had hoped to see: a child minus a little unit—no penis, no scrotum. Finally, after giving birth to five boys, Mom was ecstatic to have a girl.

And then they turned me around.

And Mom thought, "Oh . . . my . . . God."

She saw these little testes hanging down.

From what Mom tells me, I was a pretty good baby, other than my eating disorder. Up until I was about nine months old, I couldn't gain any weight. Problem was, every time I finished sucking my bottle, Mom or Pops would put me over his or her shoulder and burp me, and I would start vomiting, almost on cue. Not to be too graphic, but it wouldn't be dripping down the sides of my mouth, onto my bib. It would be flying out of my mouth, across the room, and onto walls. This is why to this day, Mom says that as a baby I was a "projectile vomiter."

Since I was smaller than other babies my age, Pops said to Mom, "Tell the doctor there's something wrong with him and don't bring him back until he's fixed." That was Pops, intolerant of any bad behavior. And I could understand his point. I was so sloppy, they had to rip the carpeting out of our house because I had ruined it.

Mom took me to the doctor first and when the problem persisted, she took me to a hospital, where they admitted me overnight, for about 24 hours. Doctors thought it might be some type of milk allergy, coming from the goat milk or soy-bean milk I had been drinking, but they never figured out exactly what it was, whether it was related to my migraines or something else. But I do know that once Mom and Pops started feeding me Kool-Aid and strained carrots—the diet I ended up being raised on as a little tyke—I started keeping the food down and gaining some weight.

Enough to start playing football. Like most kids, I loved sports, all sports. I played baseball, but I wasn't very good at it. I was a catcher and I swung at everything that came my way. Strike one, strike two, strike three, I was out, every time. I was better in basketball, but not much. But football, that was another story. From the start I was another one of those wonder boys, Mr. Pop Warner.

I was seven the first time I suited up at San Diego's Valencia Park. I played right guard, my brother Terry played left guard, and we just crushed people. We used to see who could get the most knockouts. Our quarterback would be scrambling, and someone would be chasing him, and my brother or I would chase down the defender and—BOP!—the kid would be out, the ambulance would be on its way.

By my second year of Pop Warner, my coach, Frank

White, whom I'm still close to after all these years, moved me to running back. I fell in love with the position immediately. It was a position that all the kids recognized, and when I played football, I wanted to be recognized. It meant coaches would put you in the game more, they would give you the ball more, they would treat you differently, and they would make sure you made the team. No doubt I was making the team.

I remember the first game, I was breaking tackles and running over kids, and they were, like, "Whoa!" I was just ripping them, shredding up people. Coach White was a smart man, he recognized talent. He kept me in there, and he did something else for me that was just as signifcant. He started calling me "Boss Hogg," a nickname that caught on right away and to this day has lasted around San Diego.

Where he came up with the name is kind of a funny story. I used to go over to the Whites' house and we would watch *The Dukes of Hazard*. On the show, the guy who drove the white Cadillac was nicknamed Boss Hogg. Coach White used to drive a blue Cadillac that was known as Hogg, and I would always sit in the front seat, so he would call me Boss. Boss Hogg. And for a child to have that name, it was like, "Damn!" I was loving being Boss Hogg.

Other kids in the neighborhood caught on to the name really quickly. They heard about it, and I think it scared them. I used to just run them over, that was my strength. There were no moves, only power. Boss Hogg—the name became appropriate.

The other teams always would be keying on me, so what we'd try to do is throw them off a little. Instead of wearing my regular No. 33, I would switch to a different number, like No. 30 or No. 31 or No. 32. It would work for the first play of the game, when no one had any idea who or where I was. But once I took off on that first long touchdown run, bulling over people, they picked me out of the lineup real quick. And from that point on, the defense keyed on whatever number I was wearing that day.

They didn't keep track of yards in those days, but I must have had a lot of them. It became common for me to score three or four touchdowns every game. My first year as a running back, I'm guessing I had about 50 touchdowns.

The best part about it was the payoffs it was earning me. When Pops was serving some time in prison, Mom had a boyfriend, a retired Marine who promised me five dollars for every touchdown I scored. Obviously, he must not have heard about Boss Hogg, because by the end of the season, the man had paid me about $250. It used to hurt him to have to pay me that much money, but my buddies and I loved it. After the game, we would go to the snack bar and I would buy everyone some big french fries and some vanilla ice cream, as much as they wanted.

But you want to know the truth? I never, ever, ever thought about playing in the NFL in those days. You crazy? The only thing I was worried about was making it to the next level—from junior pee wee to pee wee. As far as I was concerned, I didn't ever want to leave Pop Warner. I was always scared to go to high school because there were bigger kids and I knew there would be a tougher challenge there. So I just figured my little "Boss Hogg" legend wouldn't last long, that I didn't have too much football left in my future.

Mom says she never expected me to go into sports. She said the one boy she had who seemed like he would become a pro athlete, who wanted to become a pro athlete, was my brother, Reggie.

Me, I didn't talk or think about it too much.

The only job I thought about as a little kid was my paper route. From the time I was five years old until I was a sophomore in high school, I delivered the *San Diego Union*. So, before I started making news, I was delivering it.

Legally, you weren't allowed to have a paper route until you were about seven or eight, but we put my route in the name of my brother, James. My mom and I would get up at about 4:30 A.M. every day, arrange the papers according to section, and fold them up and get them ready for delivery, before anybody else in the house or the neighborhood was up.

It was scary for a kid to go out there that young. It was dark as I don't know what, and sometimes I would get chased down the block by big dogs barking after me. So sometimes, Mom would drive me around in her car and I would just get out of the car and throw the papers onto the people's driveways.

I had 50-something customers and sometimes I took on two routes, which meant I had 100-something customers. But one of the toughest parts of the job was—no big surprise here—collecting money. I would ring people's doorbells and ask them for the monthly $6.50, and they would give me the runaround, tell me to come back next month, something had happened. What was I supposed to say, a little kid standing at their door?

But if they kept offering up excuses and didn't pay me for a long time, I'll tell you what I wouldn't do. I wouldn't put their paper on the porch, the way I did with my good customers. I would put their paper almost at the curb. Or even throw it on their roof.

As the years went by, the other part of the job I didn't like was other kids seeing me. At six or seven in the morning, when there were a lot of kids standing around at the corner waiting for the bus to pick them up and take them to school, I had to zip by them on my bike with my little *Union* paper-route bag hanging over my shoulder.

It was embarrassing at times, throwing newspapers while I was going to high school. Most people were working at McDonald's, doing something cool like flipping burgers. Me, I was throwing newspapers. But eventually, I figured out a little shortcut in the back, where no one could see me ride back to my house and I still could make my 30, 40 bucks a week.

But being young is all about learning, and the paper route taught me some things. For one, it taught me responsibility. Getting up in the morning, that's tough, especially for a kid. You don't want to get up and throw newspapers before you go to school. But it was something I had to do, I had given the distributor my word and I knew I had to follow through on it.

The other thing I learned from the job was that I didn't want to have to work like that when I got older. I wanted a job where I could control my hours, something where I didn't always have a boss or a paper-route bag on my back.

My bedroom on Latimer was a square little eight-by-eight room, plastered with all kinds of sports stuff. We had posters—one with the Tampa Bay Buccaneers' logo, another the Seattle Seahawks' logo. In the closet were Pittsburgh Steeler stickers and the numbers of my brother James's favorite players. There was No. 12, Terry Bradshaw; No. 88, Lynn Swann; No. 32, Franco Harris; No. 82, John Stallworth—lots more. My brother loved the Steelers, and after he left the room, I just had to live with the stickers he put up.

The room also had all kinds of woman posters hanging up. I saw a pretty woman in a magazine, she was going up on my wall. I was thinking, "One day, I'm going to meet this woman." On my ceiling, directly above my bed, I hung a poster of Raquel Welch. She had a nice bathing suit on, she was sitting in a steam room, she was kind of moist. Wow!

Above my bed, on the front side of the house, was a long rectangular window, about three feet long and a half foot high, which I used for surveillance. I would stand on my bed and see everything that was going on out in the street. When I saw little sweeties coming home from school, I would run outside and talk to them. When I saw the ice cream truck coming, I would run outside in my fastest 40-yard-dash time.

Back then, it always seemed like my good friend Jamaul Pennington and I were hanging out in that room. We'd known each other since we could barely walk. When he started to sell dope to help his mother pay bills, my mother said to him: Forget that, you need a stable environment. She brought him in to live with us. That's just like her, my mom.

Jamaul and I were almost as close as family. We used to play basketball in my backyard with the court that I built. I had taken the wheel off a bike, ripped the spokes out of it, and hung it against a brick wall. When Jamaul went to the kitchen to eat, he would fix a plate for him and me. When he made tea, he always would have a cup for me. And I'd always do the same for him. During homework, we talked through the questions and problems, but never copied off each other because we had a little competition to see who could get the best grades.

It was a tough little neighborhood we grew up in, not easy to escape. Jamaul never made it. Right before my senior year of college, when I was in Athens, Georgia, Jamaul was shot and killed the week after he left the Navy. We still don't know who did it or why it happened. Me, I believe he was in the wrong place at the wrong time.

I'll always be grateful to Jamaul, and friends like him, who helped keep me out of trouble through the Boss Hogg years. Guys like Dorian Leniar, who was always fixing up cars and bikes, rather than spending his time on the streets.

And Mark Watson, a great guy who wouldn't cause anyone trouble. We're still so close that on my twenty-fifth
birthday, Mark wrote a poem for me and called it "Best
Friends."

> When I first met you, I thought of you as another kid
> on the block to play with.
> As the days went by I considered you a Friend.
> Someone who could make you mad and at the same
> time make you laugh.
> As the months went by I thought of you as a Best
> Friend.
> A close buddy who stood up for you when others
> tried to bring you down.
> Now as nineteen years has come upon us I consider
> you my Brother.
> Someone I can grow old with and talk about all the
> good times and bad times with.
> And still have fun like the first day we met.

I always had great friends to hang out with, and that's
important. My closest friends, they didn't cross the law too
much. No one was a killer or a really violent-type person,
the way some people around our neighborhood I knew
were. We had some minor infractions, but nothing too serious. My friends were loving people who came from stable
families, with two parents and decent enough incomes.
Seeing that contributed a lot to my upbringing.

All in all, I had a great childhood. When I look back, I
realize I was spoiled. I got everything I wanted—bikes,
skateboards, french fries, ice cream. But it wasn't just
handed to me. I worked my butt off at little jobs and at
school. I knew early on that if you want people to help you,
you've got to help yourself first. You can't go through life
being lazy, which, at one point during my freshman and

sophomore years of high school, I was. That was when things got cloudy, when I had no direction, when I could have dropped out of school real easily. That's why when I see kids today, I let them know, "Anything can happen. Don't give up."

8

ME AND VICTOR DEAN

Just last spring, the first week in April 1998, I flew back to San Diego to throw out the first pitch at the Padres' home opener against the Cincinnati Reds. Right after I got off the plane and onto the Hertz shuttle bus to zip over to the rental car, a big six-foot–six man recognized me, jumped on the bus, and, with a firm handshake, introduced himself. His name was Norman Quinn. He was a foreman at Hertz.

Like me, Norman had graduated from San Diego's Lincoln High School. He was the class of '68, I was the class of '90. As a Lincoln graduate, as another one of our city's own, Norman was only too happy to take a few minutes from his job, to sit down across from me, and to be one of the first to welcome me back to San Diego.

"Too bad you can't play for us now," Norman said grinning, meaning too bad I couldn't play for the San Diego Chargers, the team that plays at Qualcomm Stadium, a few miles up the road from good ol' Lincoln.

"Hey," I told him, shrugging, "they didn't want me here. Had to leave. A man's got to do what a man's got to do."

Norman reminisced about good ol' Lincoln, hard off Interstate 805 and Imperial Avenue in one of the toughest neighborhoods in all of San Diego. He talked about how he was trying to get his boy to play football, but his boy didn't want to too much, and how he ranked some of the all-time great players and teams in Lincoln's history. He talked about how much he had loved to play defensive line, even though his football talents weren't quite good enough to take him much past I–805 and Imperial.

I never thought mine would, either, to be honest with you. And that's what amazed me about speaking with Norman. I always thought I would be Norman, that I would be the guy who comes along, plays the game, enjoys it while it lasts, and then gets on with life with some kind of regular job.

"Nothing like playing high school football," Norman told me, shaking his head. "Nothing like it."

"Yeah, man," I told him. "I remember."

And I did, even though my high school football career at Lincoln was not any more memorable than his. I did not start playing until my junior year, and once I did, it didn't take too long to realize that compared to some of the other players on our team, particularly the one all-universe talent Victor Dean, I was just another guy. I was a fourth-string running back and a second-rate talent. I wasn't all-state, all-city, not even all-Lincoln. But you know what? I was having some serious fun, and to me, that was all that really mattered.

So those are my humble Norman-like high school roots—basic person, basic player. How I got to where I'm at now, I'm still trying to figure out. I'm guessing it's a little talent, a little luck, a little of being in the right place at the right time and, more than anything, a lot of hard work and perseverance. The thing you've always got to remember is that it's not just the ball that can take funny bounces in this game. Careers can, too.

Check this out. Right before the Super Bowl last January against the Packers in hometown San Diego, I got a call that Lincoln wanted to retire my football jersey during a public ceremony at the high school. Now, the funny thing about it was, I didn't have just one jersey, I had two: No. 7 and No. 18. Lincoln wanted to retire No. 7, and John Elway even joked with me about my retiring his number. The other funny thing about the ceremony was, I just didn't do all that much in high school. And now they're telling me they want to retire my jersey!

No way could I ever have expected anything like that. It was so far-fetched, it never even entered my brain. That's like telling somebody in high school that they would one day be president. Yeah, it's conceivable, but it's just not all that believable. The jerseys that are supposed to be retired are the ones that belong to the Magic Johnsons and Michael Jordans, the Joe Montanas and John Elways.

The superstars. Not a nobody like me.

Before I went to Lincoln I attended Morse High School. Morse was a big public school, about 3,500 students. I went there for a year and a half, from the beginning of ninth grade until the middle of tenth grade, and boy, those were the Lost World Years. I'd never felt more lost then, and I haven't felt that lost since.

During the spring of my ninth-grade year, when I was 14 years old, lupus killed my Pops, old age killed my German shepherd, Bonnie, and those losses, in their obviously different ways, killed whatever spirit I had. At Morse, off Skyline Drive in San Diego, I never felt like I was there, like anyone ever noticed my butt. I didn't have anything the other guys around school did, with their cars, their nicer clothes, and their girlfriends. They just had more leverage than me.

I had none. I didn't play football, didn't run track, didn't study for tests, didn't hold a job, didn't care about anything. I was just living life day to day. I'm thinking the only people who noticed me were the teachers who were failing me all the time, 24 hours a day, seven days a week, if that were possible.

You go and pull up my transcripts from Morse now and you'd be frightened. I got F's across the board. I even think I failed physical education, mainly because I never went to class. All the times my schoolmates were throwing dodge balls or climbing ropes, I was out cruising the streets, riding my white motor scooter, just wasting time away in my own Lost World.

Oddly enough, cutting school had a benefit: It left me with a lot of time to think. I kept asking myself, "With grades as horrible as yours, what are you gonna do after high school?" Then, of course, I had to think of my mother, who after Pops passed on was left to raise six boys all by herself. All of us were struggling with the loss, and what made it worse was that I knew I was letting Mom down. She was getting really mad at me. She wouldn't punish me or hit me, but she would look at my report cards and start yelling, and you know how it is. When Mom's not happy, ain't no one happy.

With Mom's anger motivating me, I figured I needed a do-over, a whole new clean slate, with new teachers, new grades, new relationships, new surroundings. At Morse, they knew I was an F student, so no matter how hard I worked to get A's or B's, I never felt like I could work hard enough to get the benefit of the doubt or the grades that I deserved. As four of my five older brothers had done before me, I decided to transfer from Morse to Lincoln.

One day while I was making plans to transfer, Frank

White, who coached me in Pop Warner and had nicknamed me "Boss Hogg," pulled me aside and offered up some excellent advice as well as another incentive to transfer.

"Boss," he told me, "you need to go back to playing football. You're wasting your talent by sitting around and not playing."

I wanted to play football, but at Lincoln, not Morse. Lincoln was where we practiced when I played Pop Warner, where I first found success and the nickname Boss Hogg. Lincoln had a good reputation and I had always wondered what it would be like to play for them. I had all kinds of good vibes about it and it was a great place to start over again.

Lincoln was a much smaller school, maybe 800 students, tops, as opposed to the 3,500 at Morse. Today the building looks old, the paint is chipped, the walls are marked with gang graffiti, the athletic fields are as much dirt as grass, and it's surrounded by thick metal bars and chain-link fences that make the place look more like a concentration camp than a high school. It didn't look much different when I transferred there halfway through my sophomore year. Yup, good ol' Lincoln.

When I was there, all kinds of drug trafficking was happening while we were trying to dissect frogs or learn long division or practice football. I used to hear gunshots going off outside just about every day. Right outside Lincoln High School today is a street named Willie James Jones Avenue. A few years after I left the place, Willie James Jones became Lincoln's class valedictorian and an all-state wrestler. He got an academic scholarship to Cornell, an Ivy League school. But one night a few years back, Willie was leaving a party that refused to let in some crashers. The guys who were turned away came back later, with anger and guns, and they started senselessly firing bullets everywhere. One of the bullets hit Willie in the shoulder and ricocheted into his heart. He was killed almost instantly.

So instead of naming a street after him for all his accomplishments, San Diego memorialized him for his death.

Another famous and better-known Lincoln alum? Future NFL Hall of Fame running back and current CBS-TV analyst Marcus Allen, Lincoln class of '78. In January 1984, when the Los Angeles Raiders beat the Washington Redskins 38–9 in Super Bowl XVIII in Tampa, Florida, Marcus ran for a Super Bowl–record 191 yards and won MVP of the game. And here's an interesting coincidence: The first year the American Football Conference has won a Super Bowl since Marcus's Raiders did it in 1984 was when the Broncos beat the Packers 31–24 in Super Bowl XXXII in San Diego. You could say I won the same Super Bowl MVP that Marcus had 14 years earlier. How many other high schools can claim that two alumni went on to become Super Bowl MVPs? Not many, is my guess.

In the two and a half years that I went there, Lincoln was comfortable—as comfortable as the pink Converse shoes I wore. Back then, my buddies and I had a break-dancing group, the Atomic Breakers, and everyone had to wear different-colored sneakers. One person wore purple, another black, another red. By the time everyone had picked out their Chucks, the only color left for me was pink. So pink it was.

We would lay a piece of cardboard on the ground and then go at it, break-dancing and getting the big crowds we would attract all riled up. And when I wasn't entertaining them with my dancing, I was doing it with my look. My pants, hand-me-downs from my five older brothers, were way too short and looked like knee-highs. My hair, courtesy of a hair-relaxing kit I used to buy at the supermarket, was way too curly. Looking back, I guess I looked a little goofy.

That was okay, though, because I had regained some confidence in myself. Lincoln turned out to be everything I had expected when I transferred. I pursued track and field my first year and a half at Lincoln, running the quarter mile in a school-record 50 seconds and throwing the discus a school-record 144 feet. I did well enough in my other subjects, and I got all A's and B's in math, which probably had something to do with how much I liked Ms. Stone, the math teacher I had a serious crush on.

Lincoln provided me with positive role models, both on and off the football field. The school's dean of students, Charles Paulk, taught me a whole lot. He would walk around campus and if he ever saw me out of line in between periods, he would give me a tongue-lashing. Discipline like that went a long ways with me. I remember he once saw me wearing my hat backward.

"Terrell, you look like a fool!" he yelled at me. "You look like a thug with your hat on backwards! No one's ever going to give you a job if you look like that."

Mr. Paulk made me understand that how people perceive me is very important. You might think you're cool, but if the people you respect are telling you you're not, then you had better listen. You get one chance to make a first impression, so you'd better not blow it. He helped teach me that you've got to be at your best all the time.

The other man who had a big influence on me at Lincoln was Vic Player, the school's coach for 20 years before he retired after the 1993 season. He was my coach and, equally important, was also my history teacher. I would sit in class listening to this man with his wide-ranging knowledge as he talked about all kinds of different subjects. I was amazed by how smart he was. He became somebody to emulate, Coach Player did. And as he also was my football coach, I was driven to impress him both in and out of the classroom.

Believe it or not, I began my high school football career as a nose guard. My first year of playing football at

Lincoln—my junior year of high school, when I was 16—I was fourth-string running back. Not as low on the depth chart as I was when I got to training camp with the Broncos in July 1995, but still pretty damn low. Thing was, I wanted to get on the field so badly, and my friends knew it. A Samoan buddy of mine, James Tufulu, came up with an idea for how to do it.

"You know, Boss," James told me at practice one day, "you're the kind of person whose got to be out there somewhere, right? So why don't you come on over here and play some D-line with me?"

"Man, I'm not playing no D-line," I told him, waving off the suggestion.

But he was persistent, so I figured, "What the heck?"

I wasn't making a contribution at running back anyway, so during our next game, the coaches put me in to block a field goal and I fired through that line the way a quick 195-pound nose guard should and I blocked that kick. Coaches noticed the kind of quickness I had, so they left me in there, saying that blocking me was like trying to catch a greased pig. For my whole junior year, I had a new home.

The cool thing about playing nose guard was not being the center of attention—the game's outcome didn't depend on me as it would on a quarterback or running back. I didn't have to carry the ball or throw it or catch it. All I had to do was go to it and tackle the ballcarrier. I always felt like I was right in the middle of the action, just killing 'em. I had tackles, sacks—plenty of sacks. For somebody who was listed as a fullback, let me tell you, I was a pretty damn good lineman, if I do say so myself. Maybe I could have been the next Gilbert Brown—minus 150 or so pounds.

Most NFL running backs are stars by their sophomore or junior years of high school, but I didn't get to touch the ball at all during that time. So before my senior year, thinking I had no shot at college football, I figured I had only one more season left to play. And I didn't want to go through it without playing some running back, the position I had first come to love as Boss Hogg back in the Pop Warner days. I practiced hard, wanting to earn some playing time as a running back. Then I asked the coaches if there was any way I could start running the ball more, even though we had two backs who were better than me, Charlie Brown and Doug Boyd.

So to make some room for me in the backfield, they put me at fullback and switched from an I-formation to a three-back attack. As long as I was getting the football some, and I was, it didn't matter to me that I wasn't the halfback. I ran for about 700 yards, and it might have been more if I hadn't missed half the season with a separated shoulder, an injury I'm still not exactly sure how I got. So I guess I showed some ability, however limited my running skills were.

But the one thing I was asked to do more than carry the football was block, block, block. I was blocking my butt off, knocking fools silly. One time, against Point Loma High School, I can remember I had linebackers stepping out of my way so I wouldn't hit them. Like they were scared to take me on, the way they were back in the days of Pop Warner.

And every now and then, and I still think this is pretty funny, I would even play kicker. Kicker! I would kick off, run downfield, and sometimes be the first one down there making a tackle. Whatever I could do to get in the playing rotation.

During my last year at Lincoln I started thinking about college. I knew I wasn't good enough to get a football scholarship to some place like UCLA or Michigan. And truthfully, I didn't care about continuing my football career. I felt, though, that football could give me an opportunity to get away from the stuff that was going on in San Diego, the gangs and the drugs and the no-good monotonous lifestyle that I had managed to avoid but that I had seen suck in so many people. If football could take me away from all that, I had a real chance of doing something positive with my life.

Problem was, the only two schools that offered me scholarships were Utah State and Long Beach State. I visited Utah State, out in Logan, Utah, one weekend with my high school teammate, Andrew Turner. We walked into this dorm, and were introduced to five dudes on the football team who were sitting around drinking. Knowing how fun recruiting trips could sometimes be, we asked, "So when are we going out?"

They looked at us like we were crazy. "Going out? Man, you don't want to go out. Ain't nothing out there." That was Utah State.

Long Beach State, though, I loved. It was close enough to home so that I still could visit—and Mom thought it was important for her boys to be close to home—but far enough away that neighborhood trouble would have a hard time finding me. The first time I visited there, I went to a couple of parties on campus, met some nice girls, noticed how close the campus was to Los Angeles, and was, like, "This is it, this is where I want to be."

My brother Reggie—who had started at running back at Long Beach during his junior and senior seasons in 1990 and 1991 and had gained about 900 yards in his final year there—was the person most responsible for recruiting me. He was the one who told the Long Beach coaching staff about me in the first place. He never mentioned that we were brothers—his last name is Webb—only that he thought there was this Davis character out of Lincoln High School in San Diego who was good enough to play for Long Beach. The coaches did some background checks, spoke to some people, and apparently agreed.

Reggie was the first one to find out I had decided to enroll there. One day during my senior year of high school, he called and asked what I was planning to do about next fall. I hadn't even talked with Long Beach's football coach, former Washington Redskin coach George Allen, but I told Reggie that my mind was made up. All I needed were the papers, I was ready to join him at LBSU. It wasn't exactly a stop-the-presses, front-page news, but to me, I was going there to do something.

Just like Norman Quinn and me sitting on that Hertz shuttle bus talking about the great high school players, NFL players sit around the locker room and do the same thing all the time. And when I think about the great people I've watched play, I always tell my Bronco teammates about this one dude I played with from Pop Warner through Lincoln, a guy who was better than anybody I have ever played with in my entire life. His name was Victor Dean, and oh my goodness! This boy had moves that were out of this world.

Victor Dean was about six feet one or two and 180, maybe 185 pounds. He was a receiver, a quarterback, a running back, a return man—whatever he wanted to be, that's how good he was. He didn't look like he was moving that fast, but no one could catch him. And whenever someone got lucky enough and did, Victor would just put these old school Jim Brown–like moves on him and that was it. He was gone.

During our senior year at Lincoln, when we were in the playoffs, Victor practically took us to the state finals on his own hook, returning kicks for touchdowns in back-to-back games. Do you know how tough that is to do? Heading into the 1998 season, the last time the Broncos had returned one kick for a touchdown was September, 1972—before I was even born.

I remember when he and I used to get recruiting letters our senior year of high school. Our mail slots were right next to each other, Davis and Dean. My mailbox would have, like, one or two letters in it from some local California colleges, and Victor's would be crammed with letters from all kinds of national programs.

When I went off to Long Beach State and then eventually Georgia, I lost track of Victor. From what I heard, even with all his offers, he wound up going to some junior college around San Diego and somewhere along the way he got sidetracked, as a lot of people do. I'm not sure whether it was with school, or passing the SAT test, or the pressures of life, or what. But he got sucked in and the closest he ever gets to the NFL now is when I tell my teammates about the best player I ever played with.

That's why I always say the professional players are not necessarily the best players in the world. There are a lot of better players out there, a lot of Victor Deans not playing in the league. It's just that generally speaking, NFL players are the ones who were able to play football and go to school and study hard and act responsibly, from high school through the pros. The players who never made it to the NFL, much less out of their neighborhoods—and believe me, every player on every team in the league knows one—are the ones who can't manage to juggle their lives properly.

Maybe that's what I was rewarded for as much as anything else when Lincoln retired my No. 7 jersey during Super Bowl week, the most memorable week of my life. The whole concept of having my jersey retired, that no one will ever wear that number again, was a huge feeling of accomplishment.

They held the ceremony in Lincoln's gymnasium, a dim place that looks more like a beaten-up barn more than a gym. But it brought back such good memories and the whole place was filled to the brim with friends and family and media—people who welcomed me back like a homecoming king. I saw a lot of faces I remembered, but a lot of names I couldn't recall.

Some people, of course, I could never, ever forget, no matter how long I might stay away. There was my old Pop Warner coach, Frank White, the biggest and friendliest man you'd ever meet, and Ms. Stone, my math teacher whom I still have a serious crush on to this day, and Marcus Allen's mother, and my mother, and my brother, Reggie.

And out of the corner of my eye, mixed in with all the people there to salute me, I saw Victor Dean. The man himself. And at that very moment, in the midst of all the hoopla and festivities, I knew Victor was looking at me and telling himself, "I can't believe this man's doing all this, running wild and starting in the Super Bowl and having his high school jersey retired." Hey, I couldn't believe it myself. And even though I didn't get a chance to talk with him—I wanted to but there were just too many people mistaking me for Stretch Armstrong and pulling me in different directions—I didn't have to guess what Victor was thinking.

Victor Dean, I'll say it again, to this day still the greatest player I have ever played with, was looking at me and thinking, "What if I had stuck with it, if only I had stuck with it, what could I have turned out to be?"

And you know what? I was looking back at him, thinking the same thing.

9

GEORGIA ON MY MIND

It's not any great secret to say I didn't get along with Ray Goff, my coach at the University of Georgia. The way Goff treated me there, after I transferred from Long Beach State in 1992, when I was 19 years old, I never appreciated. Now, I know people are going to say, as they've said to me whenever this topic has come up before, "T.D., you should just take the high road and let it go."

Sorry. I can't. I've been down that road way too often. Time for a little detour.

Goff treated me with absolutely no respect. He mistook the way I practiced and the methodical way I ran for not trying, for not hustling. I can't tell you how bad I wanted to be like Herschel Walker or Rodney Hampton or Garrison Hearst, or any of the great running backs who played before me at Georgia. But Goff, with his lack of people skills, didn't see that. It seemed to me that he plain didn't like me, and he made no secret of it. Whenever he had the opportunity, he would get right in my face, just about nose to nose, hooting and hollering.

I know he was the head coach and all, but that's still no excuse. But then, Ray Goff was not a coach—he was a dictator. He liked to walk around practice, screaming at people for all the things they were doing wrong rather than being instructive and supportive, like every other football coach I've had. My other coaches knew how and when to yell. Goff didn't. What kind of coach constantly yells all the time, like he's some damn prison warden?

Goff would get physical with me, pushing me around like I was some sort of blocking dummy or something. He forced me to practice when I wasn't feeling healthy, when my neck was burning or my migraines were raging. On top of that, I've had NFL scouts tell me that Goff talked about me behind my back, which I have to believe damaged my name and hurt my chances of going any higher in the draft.

Now, I don't want to make it sound like I didn't like Georgia. I loved it. Loved just about everything about the place. My teammates, the students, all the professors and coaches who helped me out. I still consider Georgia my second home. I even went down there last April, a few months after we won the Super Bowl, when Georgia honored me at halftime of its annual G Day spring football game in a similar way that Lincoln did—but in this case more for my postschool accomplishments. I wouldn't change anything about my time at Georgia, not my bachelor of science degree in consumer economics, not my 2.6 grade-point average, not the fun I had, not anything.

Except one thing. The head coach I played for.

Before Goff and Georgia, there was George Allen and Long Beach State University. The school, on a 322-acre campus in the coastal city of Long Beach, serves about

28,000 students. It is the Great Good Place. I cherish my Long Beach days.

My freshman year was my best year ever in college, with everything so new and promising. Being away from home made every day feel like Independence Day. There were brilliant professors, impossibly beautiful women, more parties than I could attend, a group of people my age all out to have a blast, and boy, did we ever. We had as much fun as every freshman should.

I loved the football program, too, even though our coaches decided I was not yet ready to play and they red-shirted me my freshman year, giving me an extra year of playing eligibility. George Allen and I just hit it off really well. I saw him not as this Hall of Fame coaching candidate who led the Washington Redskins to the Super Bowl, but simply a great coach. He didn't yell at players. He actually taught them about techniques and the proper way to play the game.

And no doubt, he seemed to really like me, too. My freshman year, I would get in there on the scout team and give our defense good practice, good looks. One time he saw me running hard and something compelled Coach to start yelling out, "SECRETARIAT! THERE GOES SECRE-TARIAT!"

Unfortunately, I never got to play a real game for George Allen. The December after we won our final game in the 1990 season, to finish 6–5, the 72-year-old George Allen contracted pneumonia and died.

The man who took over for him was Long Beach's defensive backs coach Willie Brown, who used to play for the Denver Broncos and Oakland Raiders. Coach Brown thought enough of me to play me some during my second year, my freshman season. I had 55 carries for 262 yards and two touchdowns, but our team finished only 2–9. We weren't even drawing any fans. In the 12,500-seat Veterans Stadium where we played, we averaged only 3,893 fans per game. And we soon lost something more than football games or our fans.

One day I was sitting in my dorm room playing a video game, when my friend Malcolm Thomas ran right into my room.

"You hear the news?" he said.

"What news?" I said.

"They just dropped the football program," he told me.

I was shocked. I think we all were. What I didn't know, at the time, was that the Long Beach athletic department had to cut $465,000 from its budget. If they dropped football, it would save $300,000 and spare the school from dropping other sports—baseball, volleyball, water polo, sports that were really popular around California and apparently more important to the athletic department.

After I heard the news officially, I thought more about the next step I would have to take. I loved going to school at Long Beach, I really did, but I'm always game for something new. This was a challenge and an opportunity, the chance to go somewhere else. It was time for me to see what I was made of. I wasn't alone.

You would not believe the rush to our training complex. All the players ran down there, splicing together whatever game film they could to send out to schools. With only so many tapes and editing machines, it was a madhouse. Fortunately, I didn't have to find other schools. They found me.

The first to call was UCLA, and I was so geeked, I started dancing all around my room. I visited their campus in Westwood, California, bought me a UCLA hat, T-shirt, whatever school merchandise I could find. I was telling everybody I was going to UCLA, no doubt, I couldn't wait. The news even showed up in the Long Beach student newspaper. Unfortunately, the news never reached the UCLA football office. They wanted me, true, but they couldn't offer me a scholarship, not at that time. And at that time, I couldn't afford the tuition, room, and board, which would have set me back about $12,000 a year.

One night I played back a message on my answering machine. It said, "Hey, this is Bob Pittard, University of Georgia's recruiting coordinator. We're interested in having you come visit us." I said, "Georgia?" I played back the message again. "Georgia? Where the hell is that?" If you had given me a puzzle of the 50 states, I wouldn't have had any idea where to put Georgia. None. I had no idea the school was in Athens, about 70 miles northeast of Atlanta. I had no idea about the school's football tradition, that Glenn "Pop" Warner himself had coached at Georgia in 1895–96. Still, they were willing to pay for my flight there, so I went.

Craig Erickson, who now plays quarterback for the Miami Dolphins and was then a graduate assistant coach at Georgia, picked me up at the airport, took me back to the school, and showed me all around. It was love at first sight. A beautiful Georgia girl accompanied us as we walked through the Butts-Mehre Athletic Building brimming with trophies and video screens. When you touched the screens, they showed famous plays of Herschel Walker and Rodney Hampton and all these great players I had watched growing up. The room had the Heisman Trophy that Georgia halfback Frank Sinkwich had won in 1942, the Heisman that Herschel had won in 1982. I'd never seen anything like this at Long Beach.

Downstairs was a gorgeous locker room, clean and spacious. It was as different from Long Beach State's locker room as the quality of the school's football programs. Georgia's locker room had 165 red and gray lockers, each one big enough to sit in. There was grey-black carpet and a big Georgia Bulldog painted on the wall—and as nice as it was back then, the locker room was remodeled again just last year, partly to help sway recruits as it did me. Then Georgia gave me all kinds of goodies—cleats and gloves and a game helmet and a practice helmet—stuff we had to buy at Long Beach with our own money. And over in the corner of the locker room, they had a jersey with a name and number on it: T. DAVIS, 33.

I felt like a kid in Disney World. To see all of this—the shrine, the offices, the locker room, my jersey—made me feel as though I already belonged. Or made me feel I would do whatever it took to belong. I was, like, "No doubt, I'm here."

As I was leaving the school, knowing I was coming back for good, I met the man who was going to be my new head coach, Ray Goff. We shook hands, and right away it seemed to me he had no idea who I was, that somebody else was responsible for arranging my recruiting visit there. Goff said something general, something he probably said to every recruit, like it was completely choreographed and rehearsed. It even sounded cold.

"Think you can definitely help our football team," he said. "Look forward to you being here."

No enthusiasm, no excitement, no emotion whatsoever. From the start, from my first meeting with him, I should have known something was up. Normally when I meet somebody, I walk out of the room saying, "I like him!" or "I dislike him."

With Goff, it was nothing. No feeling at all.

Leaving Long Beach State wasn't easy, though. I would leave not only a school but a special woman. In this world, where it's rare to find someone you'd consider a soulmate, I was lucky enough to discover one.

There was a fine woman I always used to see in the lunch hall. If I said hi to her, she wouldn't even look at me. I would be thinking, "What is wrong with this girl?" Then one day I came into the lunch hall on crutches, having broken my right ankle playing football. I had just finished my meal and was about to get up, when who should saunter on over to me but Rae Rice, the fine woman herself, asking if I needed help carrying my tray to the dishwasher.

"Excuse me?" I said. "I've been saying hello and trying to be nice to you all this time and I got no love back. And now you're asking to take my tray to the dishwasher?"

"That's right," she said, and she swooped up my tray like a hawk.

For that she got some serious cool points, and from then on we hit it off. Studied together, played together, did everything together. Even our mothers became really friendly. The neat thing about it was, Rae and I were friends, yet we were also boyfriend and girlfriend. And this went on until I transferred to Georgia in 1992.

In fact, without Rae, I never would have gotten into Georgia and been able to launch this NFL career of mine: When I decided to transfer, I found out I didn't have good enough grades at the time to get into Georgia. To improve my grade-point average, I had to make up three term papers—one in English, one in history, and one in nutrition, and I had to do it in about a week. I had to do all this research and writing, and there was only one person willing to help me. Rae. We decided that whatever it took, I was going to make it into Georgia. We didn't say, "Forget it, it's a lost cause." We just wouldn't give up.

Sure enough, we found a way. She helped me on my English, history, and nutrition papers. All on time and good enough to get the grades I needed to transfer. If not for her, who knows what would have happened? I don't think I'd be where I am today, that's for sure.

Rae still holds a special spot with me. Distance broke us up, not anything else. As far as I'm concerned, we could have been together a really long time.

While I was busy chasing my NFL dream, my mother went to Rae's wedding. I couldn't believe she got married. It was a little stab in the heart, and I don't have any problem admitting it. It hurt. But then I was, like, "That's cool, I'm glad someone's taking care of her. She deserves it." I'll always feel Rae was the right woman, only at the wrong time. It was too early a time. We both had a lot of living to do.

My first year at Georgia, 1992, wasn't bad. The running game was there, we were killing people, and we finished with a 10–2 record. Even though I was backing up running back Garrison Hearst, who went on to become a first-round pick with the Arizona Cardinals in 1993, I still racked up some pretty good numbers—53 carries for 388 yards and three touchdowns. Goff and I got along all right my first year.

But in 1993, even though I had 167 carries for 824 yards, things changed. Midway through my second year at Georgia, when I became the starting running back, we started throwing the ball more and running it less. Part of the reason was we lost Garrison to the NFL, and the other part was that Goff wanted to take advantage of the talents of our quarterback Eric Zeier.

Not that he had to, but never once did Goff come over to me to talk about it. Never once did he ask how things were going for me, or how I felt, or try to reassure me in any way. He just went along as if his starting running back didn't matter, ignoring me. It was not the way my other coaches had treated me, that's for sure. And from there on in, the relationship between Goff and me just deteriorated.

We did have one brief shining moment, during August 1994, the summer before my senior season, when I thought things might change. Unexpectedly, Goff called me up to his office and we sat there talking, one on one, about football. He told me he wanted to run the ball more during the upcoming season. I was excited about the possibilities. But it never happened. Somewhere between that conversation and the time we opened the season, things went sour.

I don't know if it was that one of the coaches told him I wasn't working out as hard as I should be (when I damn well was), or whether he got pissed at me when I went home during the summer of 1994 for the funeral of my best friend, Jamaul Pennington, who had been shot and killed in San Diego. Goff called me at home and asked, "When are you coming back to work out?" That's it. I had just lost my best friend, somebody who had lived in and out of my house for 20 years, and you want to know when I'm coming back to school to work out? When I'm damn well ready, that's when.

It didn't help matters any when I got back to school and strained my right hamstring running an out-route during one of our first practices. It happened just a few weeks before our season-opening game against South Carolina, and Goff steamed over it. He was so mad, he kept making me practice, even though my hamstring was all raggedy and getting worse with each drill.

Later, during a scrimmage two Saturdays before our opener, I went through warm-ups and my hamstring started bothering me again. So I left the field and walked into the training room. As I was getting treatment, someone came rushing in to tell me I'd better get back out on the field, coach Goff wants me out there, now. I walked out and in front of everybody—mothers, fathers, recruits, the whole team—he cussed my butt out.

"What the hell you doing?" he screamed. "You're not hurt! Get back out there on the field!"

I was so ticked off, I snapped on my face mask hard and jogged as best as I could out there. I played like crap. I couldn't run, couldn't cut, couldn't do anything the way I normally do. And the injury was getting worse as he made me practice the whole week. Finally, I figured I could not practice any longer, not without shredding the hamstring. But Goff instructed one of our trainers to tell me if I didn't scrimmage that Saturday, I wouldn't play against South Carolina. So I got it taped and jogged onto the field, and sure enough, first play I'm in there, I ran to the left, came up the side, and it just grabbed my leg. My hamstring was pulled and completely useless. I was not happy.

That weekend before the season started, on the final couple of days the players were allowed to have off to go home to spend time with their families. But Goff forced me and five other injured players to stay in the training room from early in the morning until late at night. We were hooked up to machines that were supposed to help our hamstrings and other injured body parts. My hamstrings were damn fried! I couldn't even feel them, they were so numb.

I managed to play in the opener against South Carolina, even though I wasn't 100 percent. And in the next game against Tennessee, on one of the first plays, I caught a screen pass, turned upfield, got hit, and flew into the air, doing something of an involuntary cartwheel. When I landed, I lost the ball and, worst of all, tore my hamstring. That was the last straw for me. I was done with Goff.

Not long after, I was sprawled across a table in the training room, getting treatment. There were four other players with me, three to my left, one to my right. Goff walked in, said hello to Injured Player No. 1, hello to Injured Player No. 2, hello to Injured Player No. 3, nothing to me, and hello to Injured Player No. 5. And I was, like, "This dude's a coward, a coward!"

Goff didn't even want me around the team when I was hurt. During one of the three games I missed with the torn hamstring—against Northeast Louisiana—Goff wouldn't let me stand on our sideline during the game. He wouldn't even help me get a ticket to the game. I actually had to buy one, a crappy seat in the nosebleed section. So there I was, sitting in one of the last rows of the stadium, paying to watch the team I was supposed to be a part of. How many coaches have done that to their players?

Goff also got physical with me. Right after I came back from my hamstring injury, I got a migraine at practice. Now I don't need to tell you what that's like. But of course he made me practice. And one time, when I was walking back to the huddle instead of running back, he lit into me. He shouted at me to run my ass up the field. I was past caring, though, and started walking off the field.

Well, he came running up behind me and pushed me. As soon as he did that, I unstrapped my helmet, ripped it off my head, and turned around to look at him. He was yelling at me, "What the hell you think you're doing? Who the hell you think you are? Do you think you can just walk off the field like that?" I didn't even respond. I just stood there, seething, thinking, "Don't touch me! Don't ever touch me! I don't touch you—I'm a man, a real man." But he didn't care.

Recently I found out that one time Goff marched into the office of Dick Bestwick, the former head coach at Virginia who is now Georgia's associate athletic director for academic and athletic standards, and the man I used to go and meet with and confide in once or twice a week. Mr. Bestwick said Goff berated me, calling me a "turd." Mr. Bestwick said he tried to defend me, but that it was useless when it came to Goff's feelings about me. For whatever reason—and Mr. Bestwick guessed that it may have had something to do with the fact that Goff hadn't recruited me out of high school—Goff did not like me.

It sure seems like he did nothing to help my chances to play in the NFL. Besides playing me when I needed rest, NFL scouts told me he wouldn't give them access to game film of me. Other Georgia seniors, yes; me, no. Goff later told the press that an assistant coach handled the game films and gave scouts full access to them. The scouts have also told me that when he talked to them about me, Goff badmouthed me in worse ways than he did to Mr. Bestwick. Scouts told me Goff would tell them not to waste a draft pick on me and that I would never make it in the NFL.

It was a bad experience all around. I had only 97 carries for 445 yards my senior year. But going through that and not giving up on myself was essential, I think, to my getting to where I am today. It made me stronger, made me realize that no man is tough enough to bring you down himself. Georgia, more than high school and even Mom and Pops, really shaped me. Georgia put the finishing touches on me as a person. When I came out I wasn't fazed by anything. I grew immune to hard situations and to adversity.

Now I don't have to deal with the man. We're both gone from Georgia. I'm playing in the NFL and he's overseeing a construction company with offices in Birmingham, Alabama, and Atlanta. Some of my former teammates tell me that they still see Goff every now and then. They even went to his house. He's a different person now, they say, a changed man, not the way he used to be. I'm, like, "Yeah, of course not! He's not a coach anymore! Why would he be the same person?" To me, any prison warden obviously is going to be more relaxed and a much nicer person at home than he is at work.

But then again, once Goff was out of my life, I was a little more relaxed, too. At least until I started getting ready for the draft.

My oldest brothers, Joe and James, with me sitting on Pops' lap, Christmas 1973. (Courtesy of Kateree Davis)

Me in the third grade. Now that is a smile! (Courtesy of Kateree Davis)

Pops in 1965. Mom always tells me the way I carry myself on the field reminds her a lot of him. (Courtesy of Kateree Davis)

Me and Mom in 1989. Mom has always looked out for me and now I'm looking out for her. She'll always be my hero. (Courtesy of Kateree Davis)

Me and Frank White in 1981. I keep in touch with Frank, my first coach and teacher and a man I've got lots of respect for. (Courtesy of Kateree Davis)

The Davis boys together again. Terry, me, Bobby, James, Reggie, and Joe during our reunion in San Diego in March '90.

I tried baseball, but wasn't much good at it. Football, that was a different story. That's me in my Pop Warner Valencia Park Saints uniform, Lincoln High School in my senior year, and putting the moves on in college at the University of Georgia. (© 1994 Allsport USA)

Carrying the rock my rookie year (© 1995 Eric Lahrs Bakke) . . .

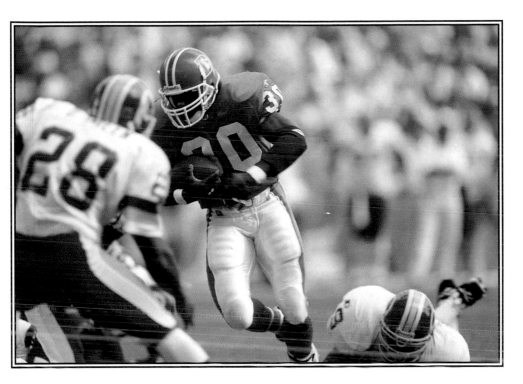

my second year (© 1996 Eric Lahrs Bakke) . . .

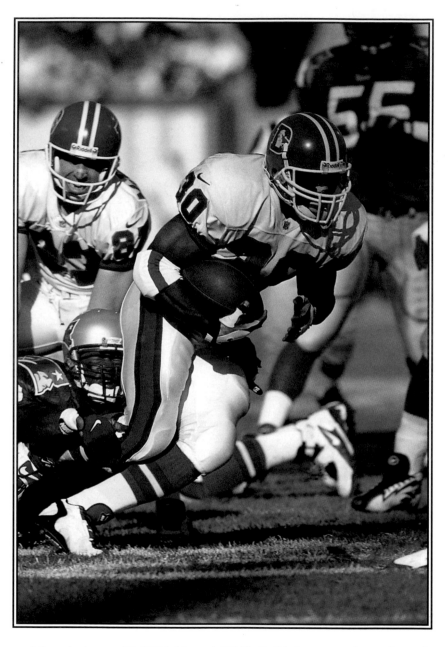

and then last year (© 1997 Allsport USA). It didn't matter what color uniform I wore—they were still out to bring me down.

Signing the book contract with my ace collaborator Adam Schefter, my agent Neil Schwartz, and Nike's Nancy Benoit. Writing and remembering all the stuff that's happened to me has been cool.

We're No Limit Soldiers doing the Mile High Salute. I didn't realize it would create such a sensation when we started it for the '97 season. How are we going to top it in '98? (© 1998 David Gonzales/Rich Clarkson and Associates)

Scoring a tough TD against Kansas City in the '98 playoffs. I felt once we beat them we could beat anyone. (© 1998 Eric Lahrs Bakke/Rich Clarkson and Associates)

Walking off the field during Super Bowl XXXII with head athletic trainer Steve "Greek" Antonopulos (right) and assistant trainer Jim Keller (left). The migraine had hit me hard. (© 1998 David Gonzales/Rich Clarkson and Associates)

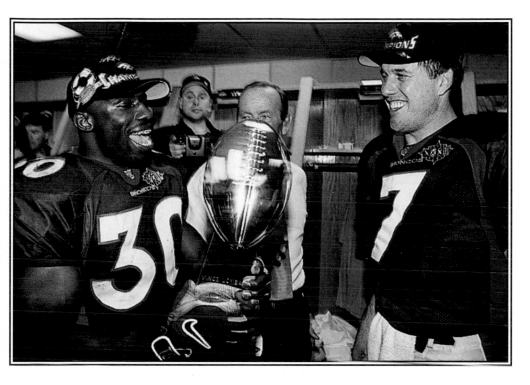

Celebrating the Super Bowl win with John Elway. I was thrilled to help him finally win the big one. (© 1998 David Gonzales/Rich Clarkson and Associates)

Giving head coach MikeShanahan a big ol' hug after Super Bowl XXXII. He and the coaching staff are the best in the business, always challenging me and my teammates to elevate our game. (© 1998 David Gonzales/ Rich Clarkson and Associates)

10

BURIED TREASURE

You know how the most popular kids at school get invitations to every party? Well, college football's not all that different. The most popular and accomplished seniors get all the invitations they want to all the post-season All-Star games that essentially serve as NFL auditions. The seniors get to meet with NFL scouts, impress them, and prove they are worth every nickel of the fat signing bonuses they're looking for.

Me? Nothing. During my senior year at Georgia, I got a mailbox stuffed with coupons for two-for-ones at the local hamburger shop, not All-Star game invites. If I wanted to go to the Hula Bowl, or the Senior Bowl, or the East-West Shrine game, I'd have to go as a spectator. I was Mr. Irrelevant—the nickname that each year gets slapped on the last player drafted. I was really disappointed, though I can't say I was surprised.

Going into my senior year at Georgia, one publication had me rated as the third-best running back in the country.

But as my senior year progressed, my playing time decreased, my carries per game dropped, my stock bottomed out. I knew that I was in trouble.

But then, the Blue-Gray Classic, a college all-star game in Montgomery, Alabama, had a cancellation and they needed another running back. And someone must have noticed the way I'd run during my final two college games and said, "Hey, there's a running back at Georgia who's got more time than he knows what to do with. Why don't we be nice and ask him?" For this I'd like to thank that person, and any of the other people who run the Blue-Gray Classic game. Anyone responsible for my invite is welcome to a Broncos game—as my guest.

Seriously, though, one of the guys who had to be responsible was Terry Bowden, the head coach at Auburn. I can't prove it, but Coach Bowden saw me at my best. In my second-to-last game at Georgia, we were up against Auburn and their 20-something-game winning streak, and I went off. I carried the ball 25 times for 113 yards and caught two passes for 42 more yards, and we wound up tying them 23–23, which was as good as a win for us at Georgia with our 6-4-1 record that season.

Up until that game, I was having doubts about my ability. Everybody around Georgia—my teammates, the fans, the hosts of radio sports talk shows—would tell me how sorry I was, how we didn't have anyone worth anything in the backfield. The coaches didn't come out and say so— they didn't have to. We didn't run the ball, which meant we didn't have a guy who could carry the load, and you know what? I started believing that.

But by the week before we played Auburn, I had had enough. I stopped feeling sorry for myself. I figured this was the second-to-last football game of my life. I didn't think I had any chance of playing in the pros so I promised myself I would do something I could look back on with some pride. That was my motivation. So that week, in practice, I busted my butt. I improvised more than I ever had. I was cutting left, moving right, running wild, having a great week of practice, and I could tell the coaches were asking themselves, "What the hell is going on here with this cat?" For the first time at Georgia, for the first time since I was Boss Hogg back in the Pop Warner days, I started believing in myself. And the coaches had no choice but to reward me.

"Look," our running backs coach, David Kelly, told me when he pulled me aside after one practice, "the coaches think you might be ready to run the ball."

"I've been ready to run the ball," I told him. "Let me at it."

And the Friday night after our team meeting, I did something that I had never done at Lincoln or Long Beach or anywhere I'd played football. I stood up in front of the whole team and told them, "You give me the ball, I'll get you your hundred yards." I got them 113 yards. To deliver on that guarantee was a big-time confidence booster.

The next week we played Georgia Tech, and Georgia gave me 25 more carries. And I gave them 121 more yards and two touchdowns. To this day, I believe those two games and those 234 yards not only helped me feel better about myself, but also improved my chances of making it in the NFL. Instead of becoming an undrafted free agent, now I figured had a shot at being a late-round pick. And even a shot at going to one of the college All-Star games.

When I received the invitation for December's Blue-Gray Classic, I had to be the most excited person ever to be visiting Montgomery. My energy showed. I had some great practices, catching every ball, running really well, and I got to meet and hang out with Pittsburgh running back Curtis Martin, now the New York Jets' big-time back and my good buddy.

Curtis and I gravitated to each other immediately. Almost right away we realized we had really similar backgrounds, similar experiences, similar personalities—modest and humble and fun. Since then, we've been fast friends. It's just that unless we see each other at a card-signing show or the Pro Bowl or something like that, we don't get to hang out with each other as much as we'd like. But we're as friendly as two people with crazy schedules, living in two different time zones, can be.

The thing I remember most from my week in Montgomery? Anthony Shelman, a running back from Louisville. This guy was real cool. He kept talking about the all the money he was going to be making in the NFL, and how he had already bought all kinds of cars, and I was thinking, "Man, this guy is putting all his eggs in one basket, spending all this money before he's even gone to camp."

Unfortunately, there was nothing sunny-side up about Anthony's eggs. Anthony Shelman never made it to the league. I was just praying I could.

After our season at Georgia ended, I was also invited to the NFL's annual scouting combine in early February in Indianapolis, where each team sends its general manager, head coach, assistant coaches, scouts, trainers—anybody who's anybody. It's yet another chance to make an impression on a team. What I didn't expect was how degrading the experience would be.

For the physicals, I was grouped with 15 other running backs. We had to strip down until we were butt-naked, walk out on stage, and stand there while all the interested teams' trainers took a closer look. One by one we were weighed and measured. The measurements—height, arm width, that kind of stuff—were announced to a bunch of coaches and personnel people sitting around with pens and pads.

All the while I was thinking, "This is ridiculous, this is a meat market!" There were so many doctors and too many lines to wait on. Then there was the special treatment. While I was standing on line with the other 15 running backs for individual physicals with each team, Penn State running back Ki-Jana Carter, who wound up being the top pick in the draft, heading to Cincinnati, walked in and got escorted right to the front. I was, like, "What's that!? I've been waiting here for hours, how you gonna just cut me?" But that's the way it was. The elite backs went to the front of the line; the scrubs like me went to the back.

And it wasn't like we were waiting on line to get into a nightclub or someplace fun like that. We were getting our private parts probed. Each team had its full training staff there and each doctor would poke around. With 30 teams—and at least four or five doctors per team—there was a lot of grabbing and tugging to make sure there were no hidden injuries. If you had a minuscule wart, believe me, they would find it. They even found a little wrist injury I suffered during a game early during my senior season.

I went into those physicals feeling fine. But by the time all the trainers got through with me, it was as if I had just experienced a grueling game. I felt beaten and battered.

To top off my memorable weekend in Indy, the scouts needed to clock me in the 40-yard dash. I lined up, fired out of the box, and crossed the finish line in. . . a cementlike 4.7 seconds. All in all, Indy was one bad time.

The last chances I had to impress the NFL and boost my value came during March and April, in the three private on-campus workouts, which were open to and attended by almost all teams. To prepare for them, I hired two personal trainers, a husband-and-wife team, Lawrence and Kathy Seagrave. It wasn't that I was in bad shape. I just wanted to be in better shape. They did just what I wanted them to. They gave me protein packs, vitamins, minerals, and put me through long, tough workouts every day at four P.M. I turned into a workout warrior.

While I worked out with them I would see my teammates working out by themselves. Somebody once told me that one of my former teammates was looking at me go through one of my daily workouts like I was crazy and it was the funniest thing he ever saw. He was laughing at me, saying, "What's T.D. up to? He ain't going to the league."

But I was determined to show everybody I could. I dropped some weight, got in first-round shape, and even some of my teammates started to notice. They were telling me, "T.D., you're looking good!" And I had to admit, I felt good. During my three private on-campus workouts, I had some very good showings. I managed to shave .3 second off my 40-yard-dash time, going from a 4.7 to a 4.4. Now I figured there had to be somebody out there interested in a back who would be willing to do whatever it took—blocking, catching, playing special teams—to make a team.

The team I really hoped would take me, the team I really wanted to play for, was the Green Bay Packers. I wanted to be a cheese-head. In the months leading up to the draft, Green Bay gave me a lot of love, not to mention Packer sweatshirts, sweatpants, all kinds of paraphernalia. And what can I say? I'm a sucker for free stuff.

One of their scouts, Harry Sydney, also gave me something that was even more significant: encouragement. He sat me down and told me how perfect I would be for the Packer offense. And the more I thought about it, the more I agreed with the man. They ran an offense in which a back didn't have to run for 1,000 yards, and I thought 1,000 yards was too many for me anyway. But I figured could give them a good 500, 600 yards, some catches, some blocks. I figured I could do the little things for them. Never thought I would be good or important enough to help beat them in a Super Bowl.

A few other teams that showed me some love, too. The Tampa Bay Buccaneers, in the person of their then head coach, Sam Wyche, took me aside and quizzed me on a whole bunch of subjects. Whom did I want to play for, why would I want to play for Tampa Bay, that kind of stuff. Wyche was the only head coach I got to talk to one-on-one. I figured that had to count for something, that their big man wanted to meet with you up close and personal.

The Cleveland Browns also showed a lot of love. They came to every one of my workouts and brought out some of their big people, too, like the director of player personnel, Mike Lombardi, and the director of pro personnel, Ozzie Newsome. I have to admit, I don't know if they were there to see me or Georgia's quarterback, Eric Zeier, or maybe both. But I'm betting they mostly came to see Eric, since they took him in the third round of the draft.

The Browns did take me aside, in private, and worked me like a dog. They made me push a sled, hit a sled, run, jump, work my butt off. When I got done, I was so damn tired I wanted to collapse. My work was done, and I thought I had worked out well. On the basis of the draft, I guess they didn't agree.

To me, three of the key things that dictate where any player is drafted are his statistics, his 40-yard-dash times, and the comments of ESPN's supposed draft guru, Mel Kiper, Jr. Want to know what I think of that trio? None of them really matters, that's what I think.

My stats weren't great at Georgia, weren't even very good. I rushed for only 445 yards my senior season. But go beyond the stats, look at the damn game film. No, I wasn't consistent in my statistics, but I was consistent with my assignments. I blocked who I was supposed to, ran where I was supposed to, did what I was instructed to do. If scouts had looked closely at my final two college games, the ones against Auburn and Georgia Tech, maybe they would have seen the same things the Broncos did.

Drafting on the basis of 40-yard-dash times is a mistake, too. So what if you run a 4.7 or 4.8 40-yard dash in a straight line on a track? Football is not track. Take the same 40 yards and put them on the football field. Give me a game situation with the Broncos down six and Cowboys cornerback Deion Sanders chasing me from behind with me intent on getting to the end zone. You watch how fast I go 40, how I weave and bob, do all I can to put the ball over the goal line.

And I'm continually amazed at the influence a guy like Mel Kiper Jr. has. He sits on the ESPN set, each hair carefully in place, and passes judgment. His opinion of me was: I was not going to make it, I was not pro material. Let me tell you, anybody could get paid to go around critiquing, even if they don't necessarily know what they're talking about. And the NFL and the media and the fans treat these pundits like prophets. If Mel says a player is no good, as he did with me, that player is no good. And he falls in the draft—hard.

Hey, what goes around comes around. Mel offered up his critique of me, so I'm figuring he should have no problem with my offering up my critique of him. Here it is:

When it comes to draft experts, Mel Kiper Jr. is a late-rounder. At best.

Funny how things work out, though. Just last March, I went back to Athens, Georgia, to do a little chillin', a little relaxin', and whom should I bump into? None other than the same player who used to openly ridicule me during my workouts.

"Hey, T.D.," he said, "congratulations on the Super Bowl and everything else. I knew you would make it, knew it."

Yeah, right, whatever.

I'll be honest here. What all those doubters out there

said back then, as well as on draft day, doesn't bother me, not one bit. You know why? In this here world, the best revenge is success. That is the sweetest revenge you can put on anybody.

On the first day of the draft, while I was at some party at an ex-girlfriend's house in Riverdale, Georgia, one of the Dallas Cowboy coaches got a hold of me on the telephone during the third round. The Cowboys were about to pick a running back, he said, and they were giving some thought to me. Before the coach hung up with me, he asked, if I didn't wind up getting drafted, would I be interested in signing with Dallas as an undrafted free agent.

When I heard those two words—"free agent"—my heart stopped. Just thinking about it was like sniffing some nasty-smelling material, a complete dose of reality. The thought that I wouldn't be drafted really brought me down. Then I was brought down even more. In round 3, the Cowboys drafted Alabama running back Sherman Williams.

The first day of the draft, rounds 1 through 3, came and went. My name was on the draft board when the day started and it was on the draft board when the day ended.

It didn't bother me that I didn't get picked the first day of the draft, but it sure seemed to bother everyone that I was hanging around.

"Sorry," one friend after another told me that Saturday afternoon. "Sorry you didn't get drafted. But tomorrow's your day, tomorrow."

My mom hugged me, my friends consoled me, but you know what? I hate that sympathy. I didn't want it then, or ever. Even though I had good on-campus workouts, I knew I didn't have a good senior season or a good combine. I had never expected to go high in the draft. You know how bothered I was I didn't get picked the first day? I went out that night in downtown Atlanta, partying. That weekend was "Freaknik," a kind of Mardi Gras for black college students, and I wasn't going to miss that. I hit the town, had some fun, stayed out real late, and didn't get up the next day until well after noon—well after the second day of the draft had gotten under way.

I woke up at a friend's house that day and was, like, "Well, the draft is on, let's go see where my future's at." When I walked into the living room, no one said a word to me, so I guessed I hadn't been picked yet. My family and friends were gathered around the TV, and after I joined them, it was hard for me to believe what I was seeing. Players whom I had never heard of were getting picked ahead of me.

I turned to the guy who is now my former agent and, with growing impatience, said, "All right, look, I haven't been drafted yet. What plans do you have for me if I don't get picked?"

"Well," he told me, "you're going to get drafted. So don't even worry about it."

"That's not what I'm asking you," I said. "What I'm asking you is, if I don't get drafted, what teams are we going to approach."

And he really didn't have an answer. Right there and then I knew something was wrong. He was supposed to have done his homework, he was supposed to have a backup plan. It was obvious he didn't. Anyway, the longer the draft went on, the more it looked like I wasn't going anywhere—except into a state of depression.

The sand in the hourglass was flowing, and there were only so many more grains left. Names were flying. All except mine. Round 4 came and went. Then round 5— which almost turned out to be my round.

At the time I didn't know it, but Green Bay's director of college scouting, John Dorsey, who was then their top southeast scout, recommended to the Packer general manager, Ron Wolf, that they grab me in the fifth round. Wolf studied the draft board, studied my name hard, but just couldn't pull the trigger. He didn't like my injury history, the fact that I'd missed three games my senior season with a torn hamstring and had some minor wrist problems. So the Packers passed on me and took Citadel running back Travis Jervey instead.

That was my last shot at having my selection announced on a television channel that we could get at my friend's house, where I was staying. After the fifth round, ESPN cut off its coverage of the draft, moving the final two rounds, rounds 6 and 7, over to ESPN 2. But the house I was watching the draft in didn't have ESPN 2 on its cable service. So while I chowed down some barbecued steak and chicken, my former agent's partner went to Frankie's Sports Bar in Atlanta to watch the rest of the draft and to keep me posted. I figured there was nothing I could do about my future anyway, so I didn't go with him.

Somebody once told me that the team that selects you is usually the one you least expect. And I thought, "Man, how can a team just pick you out of the blue; they have to at least come to a work out!"

What did I know? The Denver Broncos did not attend any of my on-campus workouts, not a single one. Still, in a standard one-page report that the Broncos' then southeastern scout Jeff Smith filed on me in October 1994, when I was struggling through my senior season, he wrote, "I'd like to have this guy in our camp because I feel there might be more here than what I saw."

And the Broncos' offensive coordinator, Gary Kubiak, without my knowing, also did a little background checking. He called Texas A&M's offensive coordinator, Steve Ensminger, who had been Georgia's offensive coordinator during my junior season, asking all about me. And Gary also called Georgia quarterbacks coach Greg Davis, who worked with me.

Gary was less interested in my physical skills than in my personality traits. He asked Steve and Greg whether I was a responsible person, whether I fit in well with my teammates, whether I worked hard. Apparently, Steve and Greg—whom I got along with well—told Gary I was bright and trustworthy—and one other thing. They told Gary that if the Broncos could get me where they wanted to get me, in one of the late rounds of the draft, they would be getting themselves a real steal.

Finally, after a couple of hours, my former agent's partner called with the word. In the sixth round, after 20 other running backs had been taken, the Denver Broncos tried to uncover some buried treasure. They had selected me with the draft's 196th pick. Everybody around me started going crazy, hugging and shouting and celebrating. Me? I was in no mood to celebrate.

"Denver?" I said to my agent in disbelief. "Denver?"

I had never been to Denver. I didn't know anything about the team, other than that John Elway was the quarterback. I couldn't have even told you who the head coach was, though later that night Mike Shanahan called to introduce himself and congratulate me.

I had so many mixed emotions. It was nice to be drafted and all, but at the same time, I had gone in the sixth round. I might as well have been a free agent, might as well have been Mr. Irrelevant. Because now, I was figuring I was going to be straight training camp meat. I figured they were going to take me in there, they were going to beat me up, and they were going to release me. Of course, at that moment my family and friends did not see it that way.

"Oh, baby, you should be happy," my mom told me as she gave me a hug.

"No, I shouldn't," I whispered to her, and I meant it. Getting drafted and making the team were two entirely different things. I had accomplished the first part; now all I could think about was the second. And I let my mom know that.

"The day I'll be happy," I told my mom, "is when it's opening day, and I'm the starting running back for the Denver Broncos. That's when I'll be happy."

11

SIXTH-STRINGER

On my first drive to my first training camp with the Denver Broncos in July 1995, my mind was running the way I normally do. All over the place.

All the way along Highway 85 driving to the University of Northern Colorado in Greeley, about 65 miles northeast of Denver, I was filled with anticipation. I could not wait to get to camp, to see what this whole thing was about. But at the same time, I was nervous as hell. This was a whole new world. I had no idea what an NFL camp was like, what the coaches wanted, what I was required to do.

Or how the hell I was going to make this football team.

I was sixth string—sixth string!—on the Broncos depth chart. I was so low on the chart, I was nearly off the chart. Glyn Milburn, Rod Bernstine, Aaron Craver, Reggie Rivers, and Sheldon Canley were all listed ahead of me. Hell, if *you* were in training camp, *you* would have been listed ahead of me!

On one of the first days of training camp, I even

remember overhearing the Bronco media relations assistant, Richard Stewart, nonchalantly telling Harlan Huckleby, a former Packer running back who was then working for the Broncos' flagship radio station, KOA, as he pointed to me, "Yeah, that guy, he's all right. But he won't make the team." To this day, Richard still tries to strongly deny this, but I'm telling you, I heard him say it. Like so many other people I've encountered at each of life's stopping stations, Richard didn't give me much of a shot.

The truth, though? I didn't give myself much of a shot, either. A sixth-round draft pick? Listed on the depth chart as the sixth-string halfback? When most teams keep only three halfbacks on their rosters? Vegas would have had me going off at 100–to–1 to win one of those roster spots, let's just put it that way.

But I wasn't even concerned about winning a roster spot. All I was hoping to do was win a practice-squad spot. During our spring minicamps, the rest of the rookies and I would sit around and strategically plot out how we could possibly find our way onto the club, and the only way always came back to the practice squad.

My impression of the practice squad was that they put a whole new team together. They had one real team with real NFL players, and another team—kind of a junior-varsity team—with one quarterback, two running backs, two wide receivers, one tight end, five offensive linemen, one for each of the 22 positions. I was thinking, "Hey, I'm the only rookie running back in camp. If they cut me, what can they possibly do with me? The practice squad, that's my destination station."

I had no idea that league rules allowed not 22 players on the practice squad, but five.

So as I pulled up to the University of Northern Colorado campus, right up to the players dorm at Lawrenson Hall, I was feeling like the King of the Practice Squad. I was

Terrell Davis, Denver Bronco practice squad running back, and I was coming right through to check in and get direct—

"Hold it right there, buddy," a security guard said to me, sticking out his own kind of stiff arm. "You got your ID?"

The security guard was just doing his job, the way I was hoping to do mine that summer. At training camp, there are a lot of people who try to impersonate team members so they can sneak in to get autographs. But I was thinking, "Man, you gotta recognize me, you gotta know me!"

But then you always have to look at things from the other side. He didn't know me from you. No one at training camp knew me from you. To go anywhere in this new world of mine, I needed to have my Bronco ID, that's just the way it was. I was nobody, nothing, and it was a total reality-check type thing. It sobered me up, put everything in perspective real quick, and I was reminded: As far as I might have come already, I still had a long, looong way to go.

Even without my Bronco ID, though, I managed to talk the guard into letting me pass through. I checked in and was handed a training camp survival kit. Inside was a key to my room, a map of the campus, an itinerary of our daily schedules, a registration card for my car. And the all-important don't-leave-the-dorm-without-it Bronco ID card.

No matter how much stuff was in the kit, I still felt like I was going to need a lot more than that to survive.

The first week of camp, one of our backup quarterbacks privately pulled aside a reporter and said, "This team's in trouble."

"Because?" the reporter asked.

"Because of our situation at running back. We've got no stallion back there. And every Super Bowl team has got to have one."

Turned out the quarterback was not the only one who felt this way at first. The coaching staff did, too. We got to our first pre-season game against the San Francisco 49ers at Mile High Stadium on July 29, and you know how much they played me? One play. One damn play! It wasn't even a very imaginative play. It was a halfback dive, over the middle, and I was stopped for no gain. My average yards per carry seemed to match my chances of making the team: 0.0.

After the game, I sat in the middle of the locker room, at a card table set up for all the rookies, just wondering whether this was how the whole pre-season was going to go. Next to me was one of my rookie buddies, tight end Byron Chamberlain, who had been drafted one round after me, in the seventh. We tried to comfort each other, told each other, "That's okay, man, that's okay. Don't worry about it. You'll get some playing time." We were not even sure that we believed ourselves.

One kindly reporter actually interrupted Byron and me and wanted to know if we were now less optimistic about our chances of sticking around. In a remark that appeared in the next day's *Denver Post*, I was quoted as saying, "If I play as well as I know I can, and I'm still cut, I'll be okay with that, I really will."

Just then, just as I was finishing this short little interview, Bronco offensive coordinator Gary Kubiak wandered over to me, trying to offer the first bit of encouragement I'd heard in camp.

"Sorry we didn't get you any playing time," Gary said. "We're going to try to get you more playing time next game."

Our next game was the following Saturday night, against these same 49ers, and it was going to be played in Tokyo. Gary didn't know it at the time, there was no way anyone could, but I wasn't even sure if I would be around.

Two problems in Tokyo. One, with Aaron Craver going

through some personal problems in Denver and missing the trip, we had a shortage of running backs. And two, the weather. Tokyo in August is hotter than my momma's kitchen on Thanksgiving Day. I've lived in the South, and Tokyo is the most humid place I've ever been. By far. It's a to-hell-with-any-water-shortage, three-shower-a-day city. You wake up, shower; get back from lunch, shower; get ready for bed, shower. When people ask me what I did in Tokyo, I tell them the truth. I showered.

But I also did something else. Two days before the 49ers game, I came within one phone call of quitting the Broncos. While we were practicing with the 49ers on Thursday morning, I became fed up with the whole entire dog and pony show I felt I was being put through, for no other reason than to preserve the bodies of the running backs who were listed ahead of me on the depth chart. The running backs who were going to get the playing time. As I'd feared earlier, I was becoming camp meat, nothing more.

And with Aaron missing, it meant more drills and more practice work for us other running backs, especially me. And our coach, Mike Shanahan—a perfectionist if ever there was one—demands that every time we make a downfield run during practice we finish it by sprinting about 40 yards downfield after the play is over. Then we have to run back to the huddle and do the whole thing all over again. Another play, another sprint, another run back to the huddle.

But with all our pads on, with the humidity being unbearable, and the sweat turning our entire uniforms into oversized sponges, it was more exhausting than anything in football I'd done. So after running one play, and sprinting downfield, I decided to take it easy and walked back to the huddle. Let's just say this did not go over very well with our running backs coach, Bobby Turner.

"Terrell!" he screamed. "What the hell you doin' walkin' back?! Get back there!"

And he nudged me upfield, as if I needed a jumpstart. I just wanted to drop to my knees. The next drill, when I tried to bounce a run outside instead of pounding it up the middle, Bobby yelled at me some more. And same thing after the next drill, when the coaches felt I was holding back. Bobby was all over my back, yelling at me and telling me I've got to give more effort. And I'm telling you, I was giving everything I had, but I was out of steam. It was to the point where I felt I could do no right, no right at all, which made me feel worthless.

I was out there bustin' my butt, trying to work as hard as I could, and not only did the coaches not appreciate it, they did not recognize it. And if they didn't give a damn about me, then why should I give a damn about them? I had reached my breaking point.

When we got back to the hotel, I sat down to try to mentally regroup. All I could think was "That's it. I want to go back home. I want to go try out for some other NFL team. I can't take this mental beating." This happens more often than you think in the NFL. You leave practice one day, come back the next, and wonder where a certain player went. "He walked out of camp last night," a teammate will tell you. "Went over the wall."

I was ready to go over the wall, too. But there was a slight problem. The telephone operators spoke only Japanese. For the life of me, I could not figure out how to get an outside line to book a flight back home. So it was a good thing we were in Tokyo—if we had been in, say, Chicago, I would have been on the next flight out. *Sayonara*.

So for this, I now want to extend an official thank-you to the Japanese. *Domo arigatoo* very much. Because of them, I had no choice but to stay with the Broncos. And to try to prosper. I just never expected prosperity to come as soon as it did.

That weekend our offensive coordinator, Gary Kubiak, came through on his promise. He got me more playing time and plenty more carries. While all of our other running backs together carried the ball 15 times for 23 yards, I carried 11 times for 46 yards and one touchdown. With four less carries, I managed to double the rushing output of the rest of our team.

But it wasn't any run or catch that landed me on Sportscenter. It was a tackle—a tackle I made on special teams.

Midway through the third quarter, we kicked off to San Francisco's return man Tyronne Drakeford. He fielded the kick, started upfield, made it to the 20, and—*POP!*—never made it to the 21. I just leveled the guy, like I was back playing defensive line at Lincoln. His feet flew into the air and he crashed to the ground. Let me tell you, I knew how it felt to be hit and it was really nice to dish it out for a change. I launched him, and that launched my NFL career.

"Oh, yeah!" Bronco safety Steve Atwater, a heavy hitter himself, told me as he patted me on the back. "Nice one."

"Way to go," Bronco quarterback John Elway told me.

"On that hit alone," Bronco defensive tackle Michael Dean Perry said, "you just made the team."

Immediately I felt a huge confidence boost. With one hit. Amazing to think about the wide range of emotions that you can go through from one day to the next. But that's life, that's how quickly things can change. In football or anything.

Critics said I had a good game only because I was playing mostly in the fourth quarter, against third- and fourth- and fifth-string players. But what was I? I was no different. I came to camp as a sixth-string halfback. And I couldn't help it if I still felt great about what I did. How could I not? As I walked off the field, there were all kinds of people shouting for my autograph, Japanese people. They even called out my name, "T.D.," however you say that in Japanese.

Even coaches were starting to notice me.

"T.D.," Coach Shanahan said in our locker room in the Tokyo Dome, "good job."

And I thought, "Cool, Coach knows who I am!" And I knew, for the first time, that I could play in the NFL.

"Coach wants to see you," the Broncos' administrative assistant for personnel, Harold Richardson, told me in late August 1995, the Wednesday before our season-opening game against the Buffalo Bills. "Go on upstairs."

Now, I've got to be honest. As good a pre-season as I'd had—I'd led the Broncos with 30 carries for 171 yards—this message worried me more than anything. The people who come downstairs to get you, to tell you to see Coach, we call them the grim reapers. They order you to go see the coach, and the coach usually sends you home. Without your playbook and without a job.

As I walked upstairs, I was, like, "Man, what could this guy possibly want me for? I thought he liked me." I remembered the week after we got back from Tokyo, he kept replaying at a team meeting a tape of a block I had made during practice, over and over. "This is how it's done," Coach Shanahan told our entire team at that time, singling out my block. "This is how the game is played. A guy giving it his all."

And Coach had given me more and more playing time in the games. The week after we got back from Tokyo, in a game at Carolina, I had one carry for six yards, four catches for 47 yards, and four kick returns for 100 more yards. Then, the next week against Dallas—after a week in which I was to second-string, behind Glyn Milburn—I like to think I proved I deserved my promotion, carrying 10 times for 73 yards. And in our pre-season finale against Jacksonville, the Broncos gave me a chance to run ahead of

Glyn, to run first string, to see how I would fare. I had seven carries for 46 yards.

And now Coach wanted to see me? "Okay, Terrell, okay," I kept telling myself. "Just be cool, just try to be cool." When I went to knock on his door, it was already open.

"Oh, T.D., come on in here," Coach Shanahan said as he looked up from something he was writing. "Have a seat."

It was my first trip to see Coach in his office, and a beautiful office it was. As I sat in a chair to the left of his desk, I looked all around, examined the surroundings for what I thought might be one final time. To Coach's right was a big glass wall, overlooking the Bronco practice field. Behind him were pictures of his family. To his left, behind me, was a bookcase stuffed with material about NFL personnel and salary caps. Straight ahead was a nice, big, soft leather couch.

"You know, T.D., you've been having a pretty good preseason; all the coaches like you. We're thinking about moving you up to the first team."

I was trying to hold in this huge smile, but it was not working. A little grin crept out as I heard the reason for my office visit.

"You're our starting running back," Coach said. "Congratulations."

"Thanks a lot, Coach," I said, shaking his hand before I turned and headed back out to practice.

When I was younger, I had been a newspaper delivery boy for the *San Diego Union*. Well, all I could say now was, I was ready to start spreadin' the news again. I had done it. I had won the starting job. It was a long process. But once it took off it flew. I had gone from sixth string, to fifth string, to fourth string, to third string, to second string, to first string. From nobody to somebody. From underdog to top dog. My dream was in motion.

I ran downstairs into the locker room all excited. The first person I saw was our running back and my close friend, Aaron Craver, who now plays for the New Orleans Saints. I told him the news that Shanahan had just told me. I was starting.

"That's great," Aaron said. "I knew you were going to start. You deserved it."

Aaron was sitting there, happy as he could be for me. But it was kind of sad because this man wanted to be the starting running back. He had left Miami that off-season when he was a free agent to come to Denver for the chance to start. But now, for the time being, he was being relegated to a backup job. Yet I never once heard an iota of a complaint from him. But that was the way Aaron was.

When I first came to Denver and didn't know the system, the coaches, or the players, the one guy who helped me learn it all was Aaron. Most of the other running backs who were in Denver when I first got to town—Rod Bernstine, Leonard Russell, Derrick Clark—I never got the feeling that they were willing to help me. They didn't respond when I asked them questions, didn't offer up any pointers when I asked for advice. Maybe they were looking out for their own interests, trying to win jobs for themselves, and that's fine. I anticipated that kind of stuff when I came to camp, and understood it. I was messing with their livelihood, trying to take food off their children's plates.

But it never stopped Aaron. He told me the plays, what holes I had to run through, which pass routes I had to run. Whenever I looked back to the huddle, he would be pointing out little things to me, giving me a comforting wink of the eye. We established a great rapport in and out of the locker room. A lot of the other running backs were really flashy, with their wardrobes and jewelry, but Aaron didn't dress the part of an NFL player. He was a sweatshirt-and-jeans kind of guy—my kind of guy.

After I told Aaron about the starting job, we put on our equipment. It was practice time. And, I realized, time to take my first ever handoff from John Elway. Up to that point, I never had practiced with John. Or taken a single handoff from him. During training camp, he didn't practice every day. The coaches held him out to rest his arm. When he did practice, he only handed off to the first- and second-string running backs, not sixth-string ones. Then during the pre-season games, we were never in at the same time. He played early with the starters, I played late with the longshots. So as excited as I was about starting, I was also really nervous about working with John.

I still remember our first handoff. He jammed that ball into my ribs, and he did not have an easy time doing it. And, moments later, he turned to Gary Kubiak and said, "T.D. has to open up his hands more, give me a bigger pocket."

And I told myself, "Damn, T.D., don't piss this man off! Don't give him any excuse to tell Gary or Mike to get your ass out of the huddle."

Ever since Denver had drafted me, I had done what I could to please John. I remember sitting in the Bronco locker room the week after they drafted me, waiting for the team's first off-season minicamp to get under way, when out of the corner of my eye I noticed this guy who I had always watched on TV—the guy who always used to beat the San Diego Chargers team I grew up rooting for—walking right toward me.

I was, like, "There he is! John Elway!"

And as I sat there, I didn't know whether to introduce myself to him or wait for him to introduce himself to me. I decided I would try to be cool about it. And as he was walking past me, I noticed he extended his hand toward me. I extended my hand back, real nonchalant, and tried to play off the fact that my nerves felt like they might just explode.

"How you doing, man, nice to meet you," I told him, as if I were meeting just any old quarterback.

"Nice to meet you, dude," he said.

And after he walked away I was, like, "WHOOOOA!" And I ran to the phone and called all my friends down in Georgia and back in San Diego and shouted, "I just met John Elway!"

But that was the first time I saw that John was a real person, that he wasn't cocky or anything like that. He didn't go around ignoring other players, even sixth-round draft picks like me. He introduced himself to everyone, walked to his locker, got dressed, and just kept on joking around with all the guys in the locker room. Like he was a regular one of the goodfellas. At first, I thought a person with that power, prestige, and fame would look down on players and always bark at them when they made a mistake. Like it was Elway's way or no way. It's amazing how far from the truth that is.

When you're in the huddle with John, he doesn't say anything derogatory to you. He's always there trying to help you, offering support. He has been like that since I can remember, since when he didn't even know who I was. And if he hadn't been, things could have turned out a whole lot different. If John had yelled at me one time during my rookie year—"Run your ass!" or "Catch the damn ball!"—he could have crushed my confidence, scarred me for life. He could have ruined me. All along, he was patient with me, really patient. He knew I had flaws, a lot of them, but he never criticized me. When I got back to the huddle, he made me feel like I belonged.

For making the final Bronco roster and winning a starting job, I decided to go out and treat myself—to a beautiful forest-green Ford Bronco, which was something I had always wanted. I remember sitting inside it for the first time and just laughing. But the ironic thing? I didn't buy it from John Elway, who happened to be the biggest car dealer in Denver.

I wanted to get it from John, I really did. I was hoping he would take me down to one of his seven dealerships, set me up, take care of me, and get me one hell of a deal. Well, it didn't exactly work out like that. John didn't take care of me himself. He referred me to one of the main guys who works down at one of his dealerships. So my teammate Byron Chamberlain and I went down there and asked for this big-shot guy, whose name I can't remember. He came into the showroom and said, very politely, "Can I help you?"

"Yeah," I said, feeling like hot stuff. "I'm interested in buying a truck. You know, a Bronco. John sent us down here."

I figured, that's going to ring a bell, that's going to make this guy excited, and that's going to set me up as The Most Important Customer of the Day, able to make a great deal on a new Ford Bronco. No, sir. This guy treated me like a stepchild, like he was too important to take care of me.

"I'll have somebody come out here and help you," the guy said, and walked away.

I then struggled with John's salesmen's handoffs. It was hard for me to understand how I was being passed around to some of the lowest-ranking salesmen. That was not what I was expecting.

Finally, I took the Bronco for a test drive, and it was as good as I'd hoped. I was ready to make a deal. We sat down to talk numbers, and I realized right away that the guy I was negotiating with didn't have any juice, any pull, none at all. So I just got up and thanked him and we were out of there.

I didn't go anywhere else that day. But I called my trusted financial adviser, Ken Ready, to tell him what had happened. Ken is a vice president with Prudential Securities in Englewood, Colorado, and he is my financial coach. He maps out a financial game plan, draws out the plays, assists me with the execution, and makes sure my playing field is as balanced as I need it to be. I told Ken the story and asked him to find the best deal for me.

A few hours later Ken called me back. He had pitted John's dealership against another. And it had worked. The good news was, we had a deal. The bad news? It wasn't with John Elway.

"Damn!" I said when he told me. "It's not with John? What's wrong with John Elway? I really want to buy from him. That's more positive P.R. It looks good."

"Well, this other guy is going to give you two thousand under what John is going to charge you."

"Two thousand?" I said, mulling over the figure. "Hey, can't argue. Get the deal done."

And we did, we got the deal done. I showed up the next day at Bronco headquarters in my new forest-green Bronco. The one that had the sales tag of one of John's biggest competitors. Sure enough, one of the first people to see the car was The Franchise, The Man himself, The Best Car Dealer/ Quarterback there ever was. John Elway.

"Why didn't you let us come back and match the offer?" John asked.

"Well . . . uh, well . . . uh, John, I really didn't do it," I explained. "I had somebody else doing the negotiations for me, man."

"Well, tell your money manager he's not the one handing you the ball," John joked. "We would have matched the offer."

And all I could think was, "Damn, T.D., damn! You did it again! You messed up! You just lost some serious cool points with this man!"

But then, this was nothing uncommon. I messed up all kinds of things my rookie season. Like the situation with my new apartment. After I got my car, the next thing up was my own crib. A saleswoman at the Saddle Ridge apartment complex—not too far from the Bronco training facility, the center of my universe—brought me into the model apartment and showed me around. It was lovely, totally furnished, nice couches, nice lamps, nice coffee table. And it was $780 per month, so I took it on the spot.

A short time later, they gave me the keys to building 8757, apartment 215. I stuck the key in the door, turned the knob, and saw: "Whoa! There's nothing in this place!" Where were the couches and lamps and coffee table I had seen? Where was all that stuff? I immediately called the manager's office to report the huge mistake they had made. They reported to me that the mistake was mine. At $780, the apartment came unfurnished.

I had no idea. Totally unprepared, my first night in my new digs, I slept on the floor.

Now, I've got to admit that my interior decorating skills were something sorry—pathetic, even. I didn't get anything from Crate and Barrel or any place like that. Most of the stuff I furnished the place with came from a local Holiday Inn, the one where the Broncos put up all their rookies. I took everything I could: hotel pillows, hotel sheets, hotel glasses, hotel spoons, hotel forks, hotel everything. My place was just like a regular Holiday Inn. In a way, I felt like I'd never checked out. (Holiday Inn, I'm sorry. I had no choice.)

But even with my place furnished, I still ran into all kinds of problems. For the first time I lived in a place that had a garage connected to it, which took some serious getting used to. One night I had just gotten out of the shower when I realized I'd left my razor and hand mirror out in my car. I went out to the garage in my undies, heard the door shut behind and went, "Uh-oh. I'm trapped." I'd forgotten I needed my key to get into the apartment from the garage. Disaster.

I was in my undies, it was nighttime, and I was, like, "Oh no! What am I going to do? Run around the street in my undies? Everyone who lives in the complex is going to see me." Not having much of a choice, I marched over in my undies to the building manager's office, knocked on the door, and tried to hide at the same time. I said, "Tracy, come out!" She came out all right. But so did all the guests she was entertaining. They all saw me, shy old T.D., and they all started laughing. The life of an NFL rookie.

On the field, though, I hardly ever got caught with my pants down. Aside from the Tokyo practice incident, there was only one other time I can remember that the coaches got all over me. It came during a Monday night game, when we beat the Oakland Raiders 27–0. I did not have as good a game as the rest of our team. I made a bunch of mistakes—missing blocking assignments, not catching the ball—more mistakes than I normally make.

And I could hear our offensive line coach Alex Gibbs, who feels the same way about rookies as Holiday Inns do about me, screaming about me to our running backs coach, Bobby Turner. "The game's too big for him, Bobby, game's too big for him. He can't handle it." Bobby did whatever he could to calm down Alex, telling him, "No, no, he's all right, he's going to be all right." And I was.

In the course of the season, I emerged as one of the league's top young running backs. In Denver, John Elway was still the man, but I was now the man behind the man. I rushed for 1,117 yards, caught passes for another 367 yards, and accounted for 1,484 total yards. Would have been even more if I hadn't torn my hamstring in the first quarter of our fourteenth game of the season, against Seattle. The injury forced me to miss our final three games while we were making a playoff push.

As much as it killed me to miss those games, I learned something valuable from it. I read in the newspaper and heard on TV how much my team had come to depend on me, how much they needed me. It was the first time since the Boss Hogg Pop Warner days that any team had depended on me. And for the first time, I felt that I truly was part of the Bronco organization.

All in all, my rookie season turned out to be just like the blimp. A good year. And I knew that when I returned to Greeley for the 1996 season, I wouldn't need my Bronco ID any longer.

12

THE EDGE

Most people—in all lines of work, not just football— talk a real big game. They say they want to go out there and be the best. But you have to be willing to put in the time to do all the little things, all the mental and physical things, that it takes to be the best.

You'd be surprised. I hear it from other players and see it myself all the time. Players shortchange themselves and their teams. On some of the nights when they should be home studying game film, studying their opponents' tendencies and defensive schemes, they're out on the town, out to eat, out with women, out having a party. Or when they're in meetings, they're not listening to their position coach. Instead of listening up to the game plan—game plans that the coaches have stayed at the office until near midnight devising—the players are just sitting there doodling on some scrap paper or maybe even sleeping.

Those same players who aren't mentally into the meetings usually aren't mentally into practice, either. They're out there fooling around, not focused or attentive. They're out there saying, "So what if I drop the ball today, so what if I take it easy at practice today, so what if I don't give it everything I've got? Sunday I will." And you can't do that, man, you just can't turn it on like that.

Football is at least 75 percent mental. There's a lot more to it than how fast you can run or how hard you can hit. I'm a kind of lethargic back, not particularly big, not real quick. I don't have the moves like Ricky Watters or quickness like Barry Sanders—that's definitely not me. But when I break out, I seem to have enough speed to get the job done. And the reason why, I think, is the little things. Doing the little things usually results in big things on Sunday.

Now I don't want anyone to think I wear a halo to go along with my No. 30. I've been guilty, particularly during my rookie year, of some pretty embarrassing transgressions. Back then I didn't study game film as hard as I should have, didn't pay attention in meetings the way I should have, even fell asleep during some of them, drawing Coach Shanahan's anger and a hefty fine. But the more I did that kind of stuff, the more I realized how important it was not to do it.

With me, I now know that if I have a terrible week of practice, my game won't be there, at least not the way I want it to be. Some of the things I see and hear about players just blow me away. When teams go on road trips and get into the opposing city only 24 hours before Sunday's kickoff, some players will rush to call some women over to their hotel room. They think they can just have some sex, party up until curfew, and then go out and play a good game the next day. But it just doesn't work like that if you really want to try to be the best.

Those players, they can do their partying the night before a game. I prefer to do mine during it.

Of course, getting ready for games is a lot more than mental preparation. It's physical, too. My body is my livelihood. Maintenance, to me, is everything. Some players go into a game with their hands aching, their toes throbbing, nagging pain everywhere. They have an injury, they let it linger and then it only gets worse. If it's something I can control or prevent— something outside a shoulder or rib injury—I do whatever I can during the week to make sure I'm as healthy as possible on Sunday. I want to go into the game feeling fresh as tomorrow, like I've never played before.

When it comes to taking care of my body, I go the full nine yards so I can go for another 100 on Sunday. I get massages three times a week, Monday, Wednesday, Friday. Massage relieves pain and muscle tension. It's the magic of touch. And I recently read in *Newsweek* that there are even more benefits. Scientists are now finding in all these studies that massage reduces blood pressure, boosts the immune system, and stimulates the brain. And let me tell you, you can't beat a massage for relaxation.

I also have a personal masseuse, Greg Roskopf, who does a lot of other medical work for the NBA's Utah Jazz and the Broncos. After practices on Wednesday, Thursday, and Friday, Greg goes to work on my feet. He massages my toe joints, rubs my ankles, and stretches my Achilles tendons.

And every Tuesday without fail I go and see my chiropractor, J. T. Anderson. I started seeing him my first year in the league, after I was feeling Sunday's effects and I knew something had to be done. Glyn Milburn, who now plays for the Green Bay Packers, hooked me up with the dude and I've been using him ever since. The man has been amazing to me. I go in there, get adjusted, hear my back crack like a car being wrecked, and when I'm through, I'm feeling fresher and tougher than a Range Rover.

And when I get home from seeing my masseuse or my foot doctor or my chiropractor, I jump right in my hot tub. Having a hot tub in your house, that's tight. Tight and necessary for a running back like me. I just soak there and let the hot water soothe all the achy muscles those defensive linemen are smashing on during the games.

And I don't stop taking care of myself when the season ends. During the off-season, I still see my chiropractor and masseuse, I just don't see them with the same frequency. Every now and then, my chiropractor will call me all pissed off that I haven't been in to see him for a little while. But during the off-season I'm heavy into training. I'm doing something each week. It might not be heavy lifting. It might just be going into the weight room and putting 135 pounds on the block and bench-pressing it. But it's something to get my body used to the movement and motion it's going to be doing a lot of starting the first week of April. Because come April Fool's Day, there's no more fooling around. It's four days a week, usually kicking off at 8:30 in the morning, of heavy lifting and hard running.

The longer I'm in the game, the more serious I am about it. And the more I realize games are won on Mondays and Tuesdays and Wednesdays just as much as they are on Sundays. I'm smarter about taking care of my body now. I'm 25 years old as I'm writing this, and I turn 26 in October, so I'm obviously not getting any younger. To go out there each year and try to duplicate your success, that's not easy, especially for a position as physically grueling as running back. You can't sit around and think it will just automatically happen. And I know the longer I'm in the game, the harder it's going to get.

A lot of people think you can take the off-season off. You can't. When this NFL career of mine is said and done, then I can blow off lifting and running, sit back and relax. But for now? Out of my way, I've got work to do.

When I'm not working, I'm sleeping. It's more important to me than living right, practicing hard, or anything else. Some people bowl, some people fish, some people write. I sleep, take power naps. My life is all about X's, O's, and Z's.

Boy do I love my Z's. Each day, while my teammates are eating lunch in our training facility, I'm sprawled out on a table in the trainer's room, taking a little power nap. Each night, while the rest of my teammates are out on the town or home with their families, I'm lounged across the couch at my house in Aurora, taking my own little power nap. I've got to get 12 hours each night—minimum. Ideally, I would prefer 14, to be honest. I know I'm sleeping away at least half my life, but it doesn't matter one teeny bit to me. Sleeping makes me feel sooo good. There's nothing else I'd rather do.

Go ahead, you name something that feels much better than sleeping. Well, there is one thing I can think of. But it doesn't last as long.

Now, I don't want anyone to think I have narcolepsy, the condition of frequent and uncontrollable desire for sleep. Doctors have ruled that out. And also know that my sleeping has nothing to do with my migraines. It's really pretty plain and simple. Ever since I was a baby I've slept like a baby. Even at the strangest times.

When the second day of the 1995 NFL draft kicked off at 12:05 P.M., the day I was about to be drafted, I was sleeping. Which is only fitting, I guess, being that I was one of the draft's biggest sleepers. And when I first got to Denver, I used to sleep all the time, even at work, and sometimes it would get me into a lot of trouble. I actually slept through about four meetings, something I wouldn't ever do now. I remember when our coach, Mike Shanahan, caught me and turned into a human alarm clock.

"Pay attention!" he screamed at me.

"I . . . am . . . paying . . . attention," I said, waking out of my sleep. I don't think Coach believed me.

But I think everyone around the Bronco organization now understands how much I value sleep. It's to the point now where if I don't get my power naps, I blame everything that happens on not sleeping enough. If I have an un-T.D.-like performance, I know it happened because I didn't get the maximum sleep.

I remember last season, a snowstorm the likes of which I'd never seen before hit Denver one Saturday in late October. We were supposed to fly to Buffalo that morning about noon, but because of all the delays the team did not get out until that night. We got to the hotel at one A.M., 12 hours before kickoff. We missed our team dinner, our team meetings, missed everything we normally go through the day and night before a game, including my power nap. I remember I was scared out of my mind. I was, like, "Damn! How am I going to get by without sleeping?" I thought I was going to be in trouble.

But as it turned out, it was the Bills who were in trouble. On the way to our 23–20 overtime win in freezing rain and wind, I sleepwalked through a franchise-record 42 carries and 207 rushing yards. And let me tell you, on the flight home, we could have been hijacked and it wouldn't have mattered. I would have slept right through it.

I'm not as insistent about what I eat as about how much I sleep, though I do watch my diet. If you were to tell me I could eat whatever I wanted whenever I wanted, I would have, without any hesitation, cheeseburgers for three meals a day. And those would be three happy meals, boy would they ever. Double cheeseburgers, french fries, vanilla shakes, apple pie, mmm. I love that food, just love it. But I don't have it that much anymore. Can't.

Like my training regimen and my rushing statistics, my diet has gotten better each year I've been in the league. I try not to eat hamburgers or fried chicken anymore. Instead, I try to have baked chicken, with vegetables. I also take some nutritional supplements that I get through Experimental Applied Sciences (EAS), supplements that make me feel a little stronger. Basically, I try to eat foods that my body is going to break down without having to spend a lot of energy. I'd rather save my energy for the Kansas City Chiefs.

Of course, I still treat myself sometimes. I think you have to. And most of those times are the Saturday nights before our games. One time, early on during my career at Georgia, I finished my dinner and grabbed some vanilla ice cream before I went upstairs to take a hot bath. We won the next day and I didn't play too badly, so I kept the routine going all season. The night before our game, I'll take three scoops of vanilla ice cream and just throw some M&M's on top. By the time I get upstairs, the dessert is all eaten up. Then, after my stomach is satisfied, it's time to satisfy my legs with a hot bath. I lie in the bath and rub my legs and stretch them and make sure there's no soreness. After spending a good 20 minutes in the bath, I hop out, towel off, and I'm knowing I'm good to go.

It's the little things. All this sleeping, all this eating, all this bathing, I really believe it allows me to be the type of running back I am. A little fullback, a little halfback, a little wide receiver, a little lineman, a little bit of everything. It's a completely different running style from anybody else's. But it seems to work for me. I'll get you your hard 10 yards, your hard 20. I'll keep the chains moving, you can bet on that.

You can also bet I'm going to give myself every advantage I can. I'm going to continue leading the laid-back lifestyle to which I've become accustomed and keep my mind pretty clear. Fortunately, I don't have a lot on it. I don't have a wife to look after, I don't have children I have to tend to, I don't live in a city where the club scene rocks. All I have to worry about is Sunday.

And the thing I worry about most is getting a migraine. Anytime I get hit good, smashed hard, I'm, like, "Oh damn! I feel the migraine coming." I'm always thinking, "Is this the one?" Like the Big One they worry about in California. I know in the future, with all the success I and my team had in 1997, I'm going to have a target on my back. A big fat bull's-eye. Teams are going to be gunning for me, and all I can say is, "Bring it on." It's going to make me work even harder. Hopefully I'll be able to continue running over any tacklers and misfortune in my way.

So far, on the NFL level, I've been pretty lucky. I really haven't encountered much turbulence. I know it's coming, though. I look around the league and I see what Emmitt Smith is going through right now in Dallas, with everybody saying he's worn out and washed up. I see what Thurman Thomas is going through in Buffalo, with him having to relinquish the running stage that once belonged to him when he was The Man. I see what Seattle did to Chris Warren, who was cut when the Seahawks went out and signed Ricky Watters. Warren then wound up signing with Dallas to help rest Emmitt.

And I know that one day, however far away that day may seem now, that's going to be me. The fans in Denver will be cheering some other running back, some other up-and-coming young talent who's trying to unseat me. Someday, someone else is going to be scoring the TDs this T.D. has gotten used to.

That's what keeps me motivated. That's what keeps me driving through March snowstorms to our training facility, just to get a workout in. I don't ever want reporters to be dogging me, I don't ever want to hear the hometown fans booing me, I don't ever want to hear Coach yelling at me. Believe me, I had enough of that during my time at Georgia.

And really, that's my biggest fear, the one thing I'm trying to stave off like a migraine. I don't want the day to come when I'm not the best anymore. I'm trying to do everything in my power to make the cheering last as long as it possibly can.

No matter how much success you've had in the past, it doesn't count for a whole lot today. I remember last season, after we won the Super Bowl, I was really happy. Ecstatic. But then I caught myself really quick. I was, like, "Man, this is sweet. But you know what? You've got to get back to work. You've got another season coming up here real soon."

Three straight 1,000-plus-yard seasons. A Super Bowl champ. A Super Bowl MVP. A big new house for me in Aurora, Colorado. A big new house for my mom right around the corner from me in Aurora. Fame, fortune, financial security. Everything a nobody like me could ever ask for. I've now got a life that's bigger than anything I could have dreamed.

My first year in the league, 1995, I would be at home and just start laughing. I'd be, like, "You're starting? You?" And I would just crack up. Then I'd flip open the newspaper and look inside there and . . . I just wasn't believing what I was seeing. My name, Terrell Davis, right up there with Detroit's Barry Sanders, Dallas's Emmitt Smith, Pittsburgh's Jerome Bettis. My name right up there among the NFL's rushing leaders.

My second year in the league, 1996, I was, like, "What's happening here? This is still going on." No sophomore jinx, no sophomore slump. Everything just being a little more believable, a little more realistic. And my name still right up there among the NFL's rushing leaders with Barry's, Emmitt's, Jerome's.

My third year in the league, 1997, I didn't find it funny anymore. Fun, but not funny. I had taken care of myself, I had learned everything it took to be the best, and I told myself, "This obviously is what I'm supposed to be doing. It's no longer some type of dream or fantasy or illusion. This here is real."

So now I'm busy cracking up about other things, like winning the Super Bowl. I know The Man Upstairs is taking care of me, He has to be. How else can you explain all this? So a lot of times, when no one's looking, when I'm home alone, I'll do another little thing. I'll kiss my hands and point up. And I'll whisper only loud enough for God to hear, "Thank you, Man, thank you for taking care of me." Better than I could ever have taken care of myself.

13

ORANGE FLUSH

In my mind's eye is a picture that just doesn't fade. I first saw it on the front page of the *Denver Post* sports section, under the headline ORANGE FLUSH, on Sunday, January 5, 1997, the day after we lost an AFC divisional playoff game to the Jacksonville Jaguars in one of the biggest upsets in NFL history. It was a picture of me yanking my jersey by its collar, stretching it practically to the bill of the blue Bronco baseball cap I'm wearing to cover as much of my face as possible. I did not want anyone to see me crying.

I was trying to wipe away my tears, even though they kept on coming and coming, nonstop, along with all the pain and frustration. I was crying and not believing what was happening. The scoreboard said JAGUARS 30—BRONCOS 27, there were a couple of seconds on the clock, and I was just sitting there thinking, "Maaan, there's gotta be more time on the clock! There's gotta be another half at least. Something! Anything! But this can't be it. This can not be it!" Shock, that's all I can say.

I was trying to convince myself that our dream season—the season that ended with an AFC West division title, a 13–3 record, and incredible hope—had a lot more life left in it. But it didn't. Through my tears, I could see all the Jaguars celebrating, jumping around, going nuts, like they had just New-York-Jetted the Baltimore Colts in Super Bowl III. Our whole season had been perfect—except the ending.

As I was watching the Jaguars hold the kind of celebration we were planning to hold once we won the Super Bowl, I was totally gripped with grief. And fear. I kept thinking, "How can I walk out in public now and show my face after this loss? How can I explain this to all the people who had called me all season long, telling us we were going to be in the Super Bowl?" I had no answers, only tears.

A football game never had meant enough to me to make me cry. And I had lost some pretty big games, too—the state championship game my senior year of high school to El Camino being the one that immediately pops into mind. But this . . . this was different. I was devastated, feeling like someone dear to me had died.

I can only compare it to what I felt when I found out that lupus had killed my Pops before he could ever see me graduate high school or graduate college or share in the success I've been fortunate enough to have in the NFL. Or the time when I was going into my senior year of college and I found out my best friend, Jamaul Pennington, had been killed. They were gone, like our best chance for the Super Bowl, and they weren't coming back. This was the same empty, blank feeling—that was what it was like. The loss left me, and really so many people in our organization and around our city, emotionally and mentally disturbed.

All I could do was slowly and painfully peel myself off the bench and march into a locker room that was the picture of dejection. And depression. One of the last people in was our coach, the man we'd all let down, Mike Shanahan. I can still see him slowly walking into the locker room and gathering us together to try to offer us his condolences. As he spoke, if you looked closely, you could see tears in his eyes, too.

Coach spoke, but I've got to be honest. I wasn't listening, not really hard anyway. I was busy saying the Lord's Prayer to myself. "Our Father, who art in heaven, hallowed be Your name, Your kingdom come, Your will be done, on Earth as it is in Heaven. Give us today our daily bread; forgive us our sins as we forgive those who sin against us; lead us not into temptation, but deliver us from evil. For the kingdom, the power, and the glory are Yours, now and forever. Amen."

This was one horrible feeling, not being able to listen or concentrate on anything but a season lost. Whichever part of Mike's message I missed wound up getting delivered to me in person—by Coach himself. Mike went around to each player individually, doing what he could to lift everyone's spirits from the depths of hell. He told me, "Sometimes this kind of thing happens. We can't change it. The game's already happened, already played, so we have nothing to do but to remember this feeling . . . and to get ready for next year."

Next year seemed too far away, though. That morning we had been at the top of the mountain, and just a few hours later, by day's end, at the very bottom of it. I couldn't think about next year with the pain of this year so fresh. All I was thinking about doing was sitting in my home, alone, the closest thing to solitary confinement there was. I didn't want visitors, I didn't want phone calls, didn't want sympathy. I just wanted to be left home alone.

But I did get one call at home that night, and it was from Mike. Later, I would find out that he had called around to a whole bunch of players, checking up on them, making sure their mental state was not one that required Prozac or any other type of medical attention. Me? I was just amazed he took the time to call anyone at all, as hurting as he and the rest of us were.

"Tough one, T.D.," Coach said that night. "Good luck this off-season. . . . We'll see you back here for next season."

I never had a coach call me at home after a loss, never. That said a lot to me, and before we hung up, I wanted to say some things back to him.

"Mike, I feel badly we lost the game," I said. "But I feel worse for you. I feel we let you down."

"Hey . . . we were all let down," he said. "On to next year. Just remember, T.D., you're one of my favorites."

As comforting as it was to hear from Coach, I still could not sleep that night. I just lay in bed, replaying the game over and over, thinking about how I could have tried harder, how I could have made more of a difference. I knew I could have. Finally, I could not think about it anymore. I was too damn tired.

Even though I felt like I didn't want the next day to ever come, I finally fell asleep at about six A.M. Slept maybe six hours—half of what I normally like to get—until about noon, at which point I pulled myself out of bed, slipped on a sweatshirt and sweatpants, walked outside into my driveway, and got the morning newspaper. With the hope that it had all been one big nightmare.

When I flipped it open, I was praying to see something different from the hard truth. Something like BRONCOS, JAGUARS BATTLE TODAY AT 2:00 P.M.!" Instead it said, ORANGE FLUSH!

Below the headline was that damn picture of myself that will always haunt me.

Up until the Jacksonville game, the 1996 season could

not have gone better. It was as if destiny lived in Denver. Whenever we needed a break we got it.

We beat the Oakland Raiders on *Monday Night Football* when John threw a game-winning 49-yard touchdown pass to Rod Smith with 4:14 left in the game. The next week, we beat Chicago when the Bears had a first-and-goal at the one-yard line in the final series of the game and could not punch it into the end zone. And two weeks later we beat Minnesota when, with 19 seconds left in the game, John threw a pass that bounced off three Viking defenders and into the hands of our wide receiver, Ed McCaffrey, for a game-winning touchdown. It was one miracle finish after another; we won games that could easily have gone the other way. It was supposed to be our year.

Looking back, I can see that part of the problem may have been that by December 1 we had wrapped up the AFC West division title, a first-round bye, home-field advantage throughout the playoffs and some well-earned time off. From December 2, 1996, to January 4, 1997, we played our final three regular-season games—at Green Bay, Oakland, and San Diego—but they had no bearing on our playoff position. We were on cruise control. We went 1–2 after starting the season 12–1. Finally, after more than a month without a meaningful game, it was time for the Jaguars.

Against the Jaguars we jumped out to a 12–0 lead. The game looked like it was going to be the blowout everyone was predicting, and it was. But the Jaguars blew us out— out of the game and out of the season. They took the next six possessions and scored on every single one of them. Their running back, Natrone Means, could not be stopped; their quarterback, Mark Brunell, could not be stopped; by the third quarter, I knew they could not be stopped. And I knew we were in some serious trouble.

John threw the ball 38 times, more than he had in 15 of our first 16 games, and I ran it only 14 times, fewer times than I had in any of our meaningful games all season. Part of the reason for that was that I tore a ligament in my right knee in the first quarter, an injury that did not stop me from playing, even though I was in a lot of pain. But most of the trouble was that we were outplayed, not to mention exposed. We were not the Super Bowl favorite everyone was predicting we were.

I knew right then that I would never again take an opponent lightly, whether it was an expansion team or a Pop Warner team. You take anyone lightly in this league, you ask for trouble. Look at us. Our whole season had turned out to be perfect—except the ending. And the one sound that defined our season as we walked off the field at Mile High Stadium the first Sunday of 1997 was the uncomfortable silence. But you know, I didn't think it was that we played badly as much as that the Jaguars just played a great game. I mean, they just threw a Don Larsen, a perfect game.

They were as big an underdog as I ever was. And just as it never stopped me, it damn sure didn't stop them.

My teammates didn't take the loss any better than I did. Bronco safety Tyrone Braxton was so depressed, he took off that week for Disneyworld, that being the only place he figured he could escape this miserable reality. Wide receiver Rod Smith told me he sat on his couch without moving, without eating, for three straight days. Elway went MIA, not being seen or heard from at Bronco headquarters for just about two months. And I read in the newspaper that Mike Shanahan, the most punctual man on the face of the planet, was actually 15 minutes late for his season-ending press conference.

"Ahhh," a Bronco spokesman said waving off questions about the coach's unusually late arrival, "he's just deciding whether to slash his left wrist or his right wrist."

Me, I was a recluse. Other than to fetch my newspaper from my driveway and to get treatment at Bronco head-quarters for my knee injury, I didn't leave my house. The only thing that helped was time. I needed time to heal. As time went on, each day got better and better. But early on, man, my misery was similar to the first migraines I ever got. There was nothing that could make me feel any better.

I could barely sleep, I could barely think about anything other than the loss. It was on my mind constantly. And then, from time to time, I'd be lucky enough to get it off my mind—for about five minutes. Then, all of a sudden, some-thing would trigger in my head and I would think of the wasted chance and I would just shout out, out of nowhere, "DAMN!" Damn Jacksonville.

There were obvious triggers too, besides the invisible ones. Sometimes I would be watching TV and I would glance into my office and I would see all the mini-NFL foot-ball helmets I collect. And I would just shout, "DAMN!" Or I would be at my desk and I would see the crystal player-of-the-week ball that Mike Shanahan once gave me, and I would holler, "DAMN!" Any football-related item was a reminder of Jacksonville.

To try to forget about it, I rested, slept, played video games, did whatever possible to wash away the memory. My family and friends also were constantly trying to make me feel better. They would call to try to cheer me up, but all they wanted to talk about was the game and what hap-pened and how we should have won. And man, the moment they brought up that trash, I was, like, "I'll call you back!" Click. So much for them and their thoughts.

Rather than dwell on the past, I tried to think more about the future. It was hard. I thought about what Mike Shanahan had told me. I thought about what he had said to the press. "Life is full of opportunities, and sometimes you take advantage of them and sometimes you don't," he had said. "It's how you respond to those misfortunes that really determines the character of a person."

Now, it did take me three weeks before I was ready to rejoin the human race, to go out in public. But I realized I couldn't keep mourning. There was one thing I figured that could help; getting away might do the trick. So I packed my bags, ventured back into the real world and headed on over to Denver International Airport. On to the next flight to New Orleans. Site of Super Bowl XXXI. The Super Bowl we were supposed to be playing in.

I wanted to see what we were missing.

I had been living in San Diego in 1988 when the Broncos played the Washington Redskins in Super Bowl XXII, but I didn't go to any of the Super Bowl parties or anything like that. And I was going to school in Georgia in 1994 when the Buffalo Bills played the Dallas Cowboys in Super Bowl XXVIII in Atlanta, but I only watched it on TV. So I had no idea what a Super Bowl week was all about. When I did see it for the first time, in New Orleans—there's just one word for it: Wow!

I could not believe the size of it, the magnitude of it. It was bigger than I ever expected. It was like the Fourth of July—in January. It was a citywide, all-day-and-night party. Every hour was happy hour.

But I did have some work to do. The NFL had me participate in a bunch of activities. I signed autographs at a Sprint booth and took part in a Q&A session. Of course, the only thing people were asking about was Jacksonville. Damn Jacksonville. They wanted to know what happened, and this is what I told them: "Did you see the game? I know you did, so you tell me what happened. Because I still don't know."

But the best part was the fun, hanging out with other players. That was really the first time I felt like I was part of the NFL, like one of the guys. Other players were handing out compliments with the frequency with which people usually hand out business cards. Philadelphia running back Ricky Watters, who now plays for the Seattle Seahawks, came up to me and told me, "You're a bad joker, man." In other words, a good player.

San Francisco fullback William Floyd, who was about to become a free agent and now plays for the Carolina Panthers, came up to me and told me, "Tell Shanahan I need to come over there and block for you. Man, I like your runnin'."

It was also cool to be at parties where there were athletes and actors and models, all kinds of celebrities. It was one big who's who. I was hangin' with the comedian Jamie Foxx and Pittsburgh Steeler quarterback Kordell Stewart, all kinds of other people like that.

My mental healing process was under way, and for the first time the sting of the Jacksonville loss was starting to subside. My mental condition had been upgraded from critical to stable. By the time I left the Super Bowl to fly back to Denver, I was much more relaxed and no longer scared to show my face in public. The embarrassment had faded, and I could start thinking about next season.

Being at the Super Bowl, seeing what it was all about—the hoopla, the excitement, the craziness—I saw how much it meant and how big it was. And all I can tell you is, I wanted to be a part of that next year the way we were supposed to be a part of it this year. I discovered I was even hungrier than before.

14

THE ART OF MARINATING

I'm the world's biggest little kid. If you were to come visit me at my home, you would find beautiful paintings, nifty sculptures, fine furnishings, tasteful decorations, and more toys than in F.A.O. Schwarz.

For one thing, it's a way for me to stay connected to my youth. For another, it gives all my friends, family, and especially my little nieces and nephews plenty to do when they come over to uncle T.D.'s house. If I know the little kids will be visiting, I run out to the toy store to buy them even more stuff than is already there. But there is one rule. Whatever I buy has to be something that they and I both can play. That way if they're not playing with it, Uncle T.D. can jump in and play with it himself.

Not like this is anything new. Growing up, my mom spoiled me. Back in those days I had all kinds of toys. I had skateboards, bicycles, Walkmans, stereos, motor scotors, video cameras, video games, whatever, you name it. But my favorite was my Lego set. It allowed me to live in a fantasy world, building cars and castles and even the neighborhood in which we lived. Some pretty cool stuff.

As I got older, and even went away to college, nothing changed. While other college students were getting clothes or money from their parents on their birthdays, I was asking my mother to buy me remote-controlled cars.

I spend more time in Toys "R" Us than some players spend in the weight room. During Christmas time, I'm over there all the time, just walking around, checking out all the new toys they have and thinking, "They have better toys than we had. I wish I were still a kid." But I know I don't have it too bad, being fortunate enough to be able to afford the things I like. At my house I've got pool tables, Donkey Kong Jr., Galaga, race cars, train sets, the latest in electronic equipment, video games—anything you can think of. I don't think I'll ever outgrow the stuff. To me, life is one big game, and no matter how old I am, why should I ever stop playing?

I believe that attitude has helped me relax off the field and helped me perform better on it. And it's really going to come in handy whenever I get married and start having children. I'm always thinking about the future and telling myself, "When I have children, oooh, they're going to be spoiled." But I'll tell you what, it's not going to be easy. They're going to have to fight their Pops for the games.

But there should be more than enough for everyone. I'm now thinking about getting a bigger and more sophisticated train set. I'm also thinking about buying remote-controlled helicopters and airplanes, things I can fly all around my neighborhood. How cool that would be! I might even like them more than the four bicycle-sized remote-controlled race cars I have sitting in my garage that I play with in my backyard all the time.

The things that I love about those kinds of toys is that I have to build them myself. I get some kind of rush when I do it, like it's a 100-yard game or something. Ever since I was a little tyke, I've loved working with my hands. I used to take my moped apart and put it back together just for the hell of it. I enjoy setting up a table, getting my tool box out, following the manual, and just putting a car together. Last season, it actually got to the point where it felt like I was building cars as much as I was carrying the football.

The only toy I can think of now that I don't have, and still want, is a Jet Ski. I love to Jet-Ski and I've been thinking about bringing some Jet Skis to Denver, but there not being much water here, I'm not sure it's worth it. Though with my birthday coming on October 28, who knows. Maybe Mom will come through for me again.

I'm not the only guy in the league like the Tom Hanks character in *Big*. One day I was sitting around our locker room with linebacker John Mobley. He had just gotten this brand-new go-cart, and he was telling me all about it, how it goes off-road, how it goes about 40 miles per hour. His newest toy reminded me of my newest toy. So I started telling him about the Ms. Pac Man video arcade game I'd just put in my basement, to go along with the other video games I have down there.

And as I was telling him about where I got it, and how often I was using it, he interrupted me midsentence and said, "Man, you know something? We're just some big old kids."

I think I'm a simple person. All I ask of people is the same things I ask of myself: fairness and honesty and humility. That's something that no matter how many yards I gain or how much money I make or how much fame I achieve, that's something that will never change, never. I won't ever be anything less or more, no matter how much some people want me to be.

A picturesque, ideal evening to me still would be putting in some quality time at practice, coming home, eating some chicken and candied yams, playing some video games, popping in a movie, and just kicking back. I'm not embarrassed to admit it. I'm the ultimate homebody. Yet for some reason, people are surprised when they hear that the things that drive me aren't really going to parties or hanging out with the bigwigs. One guy I met last winter told me, "If I were you, I'd have about eight million women, I'd have me a half dozen Mercedes, a big Rolex watch. I would be here, I would be there, I would be doing this, I would be doing that." Maybe that's all right for him, but not for me. I'd much rather hang out at my own house, be in my own little world, taking power naps and marinating.

Marinating? Yeah, I guess I should explain that. You know how when you want to cook a steak, the day before you let it just sit in a big bowl of sauce in your refrigerator, hanging out—getting tender? Well, when I'm doing the same thing as your steak, just sitting around my house, lying there like a big piece of meat, I'm marinating. Nothing I like more.

The place I like to marinate most is in my little movie room, which is down in my basement, off to the side like a hidden room. With a big screen in it, practically covering one full wall, I can have my own little private showings of my favorite movies. It's really convenient because I spend a lot of time watching movies—at least three, four a week—but I don't too much like going to theaters.

In a movie theater I can't talk, can't get popcorn in the middle of the movie without missing something, can't rewind to the lines and parts I missed. And I can't stand having to get up and drive home if I've fallen asleep during the movie. Did that last spring when I was watching *U.S. Marshals*. Fell right asleep, woke up when the final credits were rolling and had to regroup for the retreat home. That was not a fun night out.

I like my movie room so much that a lot of times, I'll

just take my phone, blanket, and pillow and go in there to chill. Many times I'll even take a patented T.D. power nap in there. To me, that's entertainment.

I also make sure I have enough high-tech toys to entertain myself on all these road trips I have to take. Everywhere I go, I carry around a black leather duffel bag that has all kinds of goodies inside. My favorite is my video Walkman, which is a little TV-VCR that plays eight-millimeter tapes. In March, when I was taping this segment of the sitcom *Arli$$* that wound up airing on HBO in late June, I noticed that one of the cameramen had the coolest-looking video Walkman I had ever seen. I was, like, "Man, that's sweet, where can I get myself one of these things?" He wasn't sure, but after one day back in Denver I found myself one. No way I wouldn't.

Now this thing goes on all my road trips with me, like a spouse. I settle into my airplane seat, put on the head phones, and I can watch TV, play a movie, do whatever I want. One of the last trips I made, out to New York, I watched *The Lion King* and just sat there humming "Hakuna Matata" to myself. And when my eyes are feeling too lazy to watch TV or a movie, no problem. I just reach inside the black duffel bag, put away the video Walkman, and pull out my headphones and mini-CD player. Not too long ago, Sony came out with portable, vibration-proof minidiscs that you actually can record on, and I'm loving these things the way I love my remote-controlled cars. I sit at home for hours, making up discs of all my favorite songs.

I have my soft, romantic discs with all kinds of R&B on there that I call my "Love Jones" discs, and I have my rap CDs that I call my "Hip-Hop Volume 1" and "Volume 2" and "Volume 3" discs, to however many volumes I have, which is a whole lot. That music to me is essential. I make it so that I can feel at home wherever I am. I even have a CD-to-cassette adapter so that when I'm traveling and I get in my rental car, I can just pop in the adapter and play my minidiscs. That way I don't miss a beat. I stay right in tune.

For all the toys I play with, for all the movies I watch, for all the music I listen to, I don't think there are any toys I play with as much as my video games. Man, I'm a video-game-aholic. And not only do I play them, but I'm actually *in* video games.

In the GameDay football game, I'm the Denver Broncos' featured running back, like in real life. It's a thrill playing myself on a video game, to hear, "Davis runs 27 yards!" I play myself all the time and I'll have 3,100 yards or 4,600 yards in a season and just crush all the records. One time I was even "Player of the Week" nine out of the 16 weeks. But in real life, it just doesn't happen that way. Still, it's fun to live your fantasies vicariously through video games and do the things that you know you will probably never do.

The downside is, sometimes even these video-game manufacturers underestimate my skills and don't give me the proper level of attributes. They don't make my hands good enough or they don't make me fast enough and it's to the point where I'll get mad at myself sometimes. It's, like, "Ahhh, that's unlike you, T.D., that's unlike you to get tackled like that from behind." Otherwise I'd have more yards than the machine could count.

When it comes to those video games, I've also developed some serious superstitions. Back during the 1996 season, I noticed that whenever I played the same football matchup I would be playing in real life on Sunday—say, the Broncos versus the Raiders—what happened on the video game would happen again on Sunday. If I beat the Raiders in the video-game matchup during the week, then we would beat the Raiders in the real game on Sunday. If I lost during the week, we would lose on Sunday. It was uncanny.

That season I had a 13–3 GameDay football record with losses to Kansas City, Green Bay, and San Diego, and our team had the exact same 13–3 regular-season record with the exact same losses to Kansas City, Green Bay, and San Diego. I was spooked. So during the play-offs, I quit "GameDay," and decided I couldn't do it anymore. And during the 1997 regular season, I didn't play GameDay, not once.

But then, the week before the Super Bowl, while we were in San Diego, I got a call from the GameDay people. They had a matchup that they were billing as "The Game Before the Game." They had asked Green Bay Packer wide receiver Robert Brooks to be in it, and they asked me as well. So I'm thinking, "Okay, I'll play as long as I'm not playing Denver and Robert's not playing Green Bay, and we can both just pick our own teams." And I agreed to do it.

On the Thursday before the Super Bowl, right after I finished up an interview with the NBC pre-game show host Greg Gumbel, the GameDay people sent over a limo to pick me up. I got into the car and asked the GameDay rep which team I could play. He didn't even give me an option.

"We already have it set up," the guy said. "You're Denver and he's the Green Bay Pack—"

"Hold on, hold on," I said in fear. "I'm not playing Denver. I can't, man."

"Too late," he told me. "It's already there waiting for you."

Well, let me tell you, right there and then I was having an anxiety attack. This was my worst nightmare coming true. I had to play this stupid little game before The Game and I hadn't practiced in months, since last June, and I knew Robert Brooks was going to kick my butt. And if I lost, then I was knew the Broncos were going to lose on Sunday, too. I know it sounds stupid, but that is what I was thinking. When it comes to any game, I'm always looking for historical edges, superstitious edges, any edge I can find.

This time, it looked like all the edges were Robert's. When we got to the park where the game was set up, with a big crowd on hand to watch, Robert already was there. He had been practicing for about 30 minutes—30 minutes more than me. As I hopped on the console, everyone was trying to talk to me, offer me tips. But I wasn't listening. I was too nervous. I get butterflies anytime I play anyone in anything, a video game or a real football game, and this time the butterflies were fluttering like crazy. They got even worse when Robert took the opening kickoff and marched down the field. But he missed his field goal, and from there, the game was all mine.

I led 7–0 at halftime, 14–0 after the third quarter, and wound up thumping him 20–0. I heard one of the fans shout, "Yeah, Robert, it's just a video game, it'll be different on Sunday." And Robert said something himself, something about how they were going to beat us on Sunday, showing no respect at all. But it didn't matter what Robert or any fan said, because I had an extra boost of confidence. I knew the truth. The truth was: We were in! I was, like, "We're going to win the big one, baby!"

Now I don't want to brag or anything, but I tell people all the time that that was the key to our winning the Super Bowl. No doubt. The game before The Game. Me beating Robert Brooks.

15

THE REVENGE TOUR

I don't mind the shots huge defensive linemen give me. But I can't stand the ones I get from our doctors. They're more painful than you want to know.

They pull out a big, long needle, their weapon of choice. You can close your eyes, not even watch it, but what's the difference? You can feel it anyway. And when they put it into you, they do it nice and slow, and twist it around and around. They twist, you shout. That's just how it works in the NFL. I'd rather go through two-a-day practices in 100-degree heat any day.

We can sit here all day long and talk about how memorable the 1998 playoffs were, how much fun it was to go on a Revenge Tour that pitted us against Jacksonville, and then took us to Kansas City and Pittsburgh—two teams that had beaten us one month earlier, in December—before winding up in San Diego against Green Bay. Anytime you play a full month and don't lose it's fun—how could it not be? But it was not all about fun to me. To me, the playoffs were a sore subject; they were about not letting pain affect my game.

I had to fight through a separated shoulder, a migraine headache, and bruised ribs, not to mention all those linemen and linebackers playing like there was a bounty on my head. And I had to do it all through the playoffs, from the first game on. I'm not complaining, not at all, that's not my style. You play, and you play with pain. But the next time a fan watches a game, I want him to think about something. About midway through the season, and especially the playoffs, our bodies start feeling a whole lot like corpses. We feel like dead men playing. We're brittle, sore, beat up. It's tough to even walk. And the longer the season lasts, the worse it gets, believe me. You ever need to find me in January, you can start by checking in the whirlpool.

I might be 25 years old, but my body—any football player's body, really—tells me I'm a whole lot older. And in the playoffs, I felt like a real senior citizen—without being able to get any of those movie discounts. On the other hand, let's just say the playoffs had more drama than any movie I've ever seen.

In the third quarter of our playoff opener against Jacksonville, with our team holding a 21–17 lead, I broke around left end and right up our sideline. Man, there's nothing like having the ball and the game in your hands. You feel like you can run forever. I didn't go forever, but I did go for 59 yards, all the way to the Jaguars' 13-yard line. At which point one of Jacksonville's safeties, Travis Davis, came crashing down on me and I went down hard on the ball.

I didn't think it was anything serious at first, but when I got to my knees, all I could feel was a sharp pain shooting through my midsection. "My ribs, my ribs," I kept telling myself. "Something's not right." I went to our sideline, and when I tried to get up off our bench, I couldn't move from the pain. It was a knife in my ribs, shortness of breath, nasty pain.

The Bronco training staff didn't waste any time. They wanted me back in the game—pronto. So they whisked me to the locker room right away, checked it out and made sure my ribs weren't cracked. Fortunately, they weren't, even though I was still having trouble breathing, a lot of trouble. But I had even more trouble when I looked up and saw what the doctor was holding as he was approaching me. A needle. A big, long needle.

It was some type of painkiller, though I still don't know exactly what the hell was in that needle, and I don't want to. All I know is he stuck it in slowly, and twisted it around and around. This was all new to me. Up until the playoffs, I never had to get an injection for a football game—not at Lincoln High School, not at Long Beach State, not at Georgia and so far not with the Broncos. This was my first. But it would not be my last. I also had one of those shots for the divisional playoff game against Kansas City and one for the AFC Championship game in Pittsburgh. That's three shots of painkillers during the playoffs. Three times as many shots as I had ever taken to play in a football game. But at least they allowed me to give out some of my own.

I remember pulling aside a *Denver Post* reporter the week training camp opened and telling him the dream I kept having, the one where the Denver Broncos were in the Super Bowl. Not only in it, but winning it. I told the reporter, "Why not us?" This was not some training-camp hallucination, due to too many head blows. This what was I really believed.

Sure enough, the next day, there in the *Denver Post*, was a caricature of me dreaming about the Vince Lombardi Trophy, wearing a sly little smirk on my face. I liked the cartoon so much, I saved one at home. And when I got home from the Super Bowl and inadvertently stumbled across the picture, having completely forgotten about it, I started cracking up, thought it was too funny. Growing up, everyone used to call me Boss Hogg, but feel free to call me Nostradamus if you want.

But this Bronco team was not going to be denied the way last year's had been. Last year we read in all the newspapers and magazines that we were locks for the Super Bowl, and we believed it. This year we read in all the newspapers and magazines that we weren't locks, weren't even favorites, and we refused to believe it. The moral here? Pretty simple, really. Unless it's my autobiography, don't believe everything you read.

This Bronco team had a quiet confidence about it, and a feistiness. I can still remember in the practices before each of the playoff games we had scrappy little fights between offensive and defensive linemen. Offensive tackle Tony Jones versus defensive tackle David Richie, guard Brian Habib versus defensive tackle Keith Traylor. It meant we didn't need any more practice time. We were ready to get out there and club somebody.

Maybe our 12–4 regular-season record last year wasn't as good as the 13–3 record we put up during the 1996 season, when we won the AFC West and home-field advantage throughout the playoffs. But the Super Bowl team was physically stronger and mentally tougher than the one the Jaguars had stunned 30–27 in January 1997, that much I can tell you.

All along, I had confidence that we could pull it off. In the days leading up to the Jacksonville game, I kept giving the guys my own little pep talk. I walked up to our defensive end Alfred Williams one day and told him, "Whatever you do, just get me to San Diego, just get me to the Super Bowl. You get me to San Diego," I promised, "I'll take you home."

But before we went anywhere in the playoffs, we first had to beat the Jaguars, the same Jaguars that had caused me, my team, and my city so much suffering only one year earlier. No easy task, beating the Jags, but this time it was all about unfinished business. All the off-season lifting and running, all the minicamps and training camp, all the regular-season practices and games, it was all for this: another shot at the Jaguars.

Everybody was raring to go—except me. Mentally I was ready; physically I wasn't. Two weeks earlier, in a nationally televised Monday night game in San Francisco against the 49ers, a game we lost 34–17, I separated my right shoulder. A bunch of 49ers piled on me after I'd caught a screen pass, and that was it. I was done for the night and for our final regular-season game against the San Diego Chargers.

The injury was not as severe as the one 49ers wide receiver Jerry Rice suffered the same night, tearing up the knee he had spent three months rehabbing. But it was severe enough to knock me out of the game, out of the race for the NFL's rushing title, and out of any chance I had for a 2,000-yard season. It also came on the same night we were officially knocked out of the race for the AFC West division title. So if anything good came out of our final loss of the season, it was this: Right then, we could start thinking playoffs, shifting our focus from the regular season to the post-season. And the focus around Denver—like the chip I had been carrying around for Jacksonville—was on my shoulder.

There were medical updates on the condition of my shoulder every day, whether I was doubtful or questionable or probable. Seemed like you hardly knew if you were reading the *Denver Post* or the *American Medical Journal*. But let me tell you, there was no way I was missing that game against the Jaguars, even if they had to give me 100 injections. You don't spend a full year obsessing about one game, one team, and then decide you're too sore to go.

Of course, I've also got to admit that I was not sure how my shoulder was going to respond, and neither was our coach, Mike Shanahan. But he sure didn't waste any time finding out. On our first play of the game, he called, "Fourteen"—a running play for me up the middle. I took the ball from our quarterback John Elway, charged full speed ahead, and lowered my shoulder right smack into any Jaguar in my way. I gained only three yards but I gained the confidence that my arm was not going to give me any problems.

It turned out to be a long day for the Jaguars, especially for their defense. Our offensive line opened up enough holes for me to run for 184 yards, and they could have gotten me 250, easy. My backup, Derek Loville, ran for another 103. And as a team we finished with a team-record 310 rushing yards. The strangest thing was, we had one lead-draw play we could run to the right or left—"Fox Two" went to the right, "Fox Three" went to the left. Whichever way it went, it didn't matter. They could not stop it.

I'm telling you, we must have run that same play nine, ten times, which is unheard of in the NFL. Usually you don't run the same play in the same game more than once or twice—any more than that can be embarrassing to a defense. But we just kept running "Fox Two" and "Fox Three" over and over. It was almost as if the play became our own little redemption song. I knew we ran it a lot, but I could not believe how much it actually was until after the game, when I was sitting in the training room—ice packs covering the bruised ribs that knocked me out of the game in the third quarter—watching the game highlights that were leading all the TV newscasts in Denver.

Half my runs came off one of those two Fox plays, including the 59-yard run during which I bruised my ribs.

Derek's 25-yard touchdown run, the one where he ran right up the middle before breaking outside and going right down the right sideline, came on "Fox Two." Man, it had to be humiliating for Jacksonville. But let me tell you, we could relate. On the first Saturday in 1997, the Jaguars beat us 30–27. On the last Saturday in 1997, we beat them 42–17.

We outfoxed them. Ran them right out of town. And ran ourselves right into an AFC divisional playoff showdown against the Kansas City Chiefs.

As much I feared needles, I feared playing the Chiefs more. To me, they were the best team in football, and they proved it during the regular season. They thumped the 49ers 44–9. They finished with the best record in the AFC. They were monsters.

I had some serious reservations about our chances in this game. Good teams always think that they'll win, 100 percent guaranteed, that they cannot lose. I thought that way for every one of our games during the regular season, but this one was different. I estimated our chances of beating the Chiefs at about 80 percent, tops. I honestly didn't know whether we could beat them, that's how tough they were.

On top of that, we had to beat them in Kansas City, in that noise factory they call Arrowhead Stadium. Most players think it's the loudest stadium in the league. It's so loud you can't hear yourself talk, even if you're screaming. And the Chiefs hadn't lost a single game at home all season, including the November one during which they beat us 24–22 on the final play of the game, with a 54-yard Pete Stoyanovich field goal.

Why not us? I asked during the summer. Why not them? I asked in December.

I believed, though, that if we beat Kansas City, we were going Super Bowling, all the way. The game against Kansas

City was the game that, to me, was going to determine who was going to be the world champ. I knew the winner still would have to beat the Steelers, then either the 49ers or Packers, whichever team won the NFC Championship, but that didn't faze me. I really believed the Chiefs were the toughest team we were going to have to play in the post-season.

The other tough thing about the Chiefs' game? My ribs. They were just not cooperating, not showing a whole lot of improvement in the eight days since we'd played Jacksonville. My shoulder felt all right at that point, but my ribs didn't. I really wasn't sure how they were going to hold up or whether I could make it through the game. I took a shot before the game, put on a flak jacket during it, but the jacket protected no better than your ordinary wind-breaker. The Chiefs went after my ribs like they were the blue-plate special of the day, and it ate away at me.

On our seventh play of the game, a handoff around right end, I fumbled. Fortunately, I was able to get the ball back for a loss of two yards. One quarter and three series later, near the end of the first half, on a routine run up the middle, I fumbled again. Managed to get that one back, too, but when I walked, head down, back to the sideline, Coach Shanahan was waiting for me with a glare.

"T.D., T.D.!" Coach Shanahan shouted. "You all right?" In the three years I had played for this man, he had never talked to me like this. He was asking me if I was all right, but it was not what he meant. He was really saying, "Why in the hell are you not holding on to the football?" And he wanted an answer.

"Yeah, I'm all right," I said, both of us knowing this was one big lie.

As I headed back onto the field for the next series, I was one angry young man. He knew I was hurt. I was hurting something bad. But as I thought about what Coach said, it made me realize something else. In life, you have no one to blame but yourself. You have to know who is responsible. You are, at all times. I was the one who fumbled, I was the one who almost lost the ball, I was the one who was costing my team the game. And that brought me back home. As I stepped back in the huddle, I was thinking, "Quit worrying about your ribs. Stop acting like a baby. Just play the game."

Which is exactly what I did. First play back in the game, I go up the middle, one yard, for the first touchdown of the game. Scored my second touchdown, which accounts for our only 14 points of the game, on the fifth play of the fourth quarter. And finished the game with 101 rushing yards—24 more than the whole Chiefs team combined. I might have had the most tender ribs in all of Kansas City, but, yeah, I was all right.

How could I not be? As far as I was concerned, we had beaten the best team in all of football 14–10. It wasn't something you wanted to hang in an art museum or anything like that, but it was good enough. It was a win.

On to the AFC Championship game. On to Pittsburgh.

As we walked into Three Rivers Stadium in Pittsburgh on January 11, 1998, a mob of fans decked out in Steeler black and gold were waiting for us, pointing at us, cursing at us, making obscene gestures at us. Talking crazy.

"Broncos suck!"

"No way, El-way!"

"Going down hard, T.D.!"

We walked past the security guards, up the tunnel, and onto the field and all I could think was, "Can't wait to see what these fans look like after the game." And the fans weren't the only ones who were loud and obnoxious. So were some of the Steelers—mainly one linebacker who had a really big mouth. As we're standing across the line of scrimmage on the game's first series, he was staring right at me, making a fist, and banging his ribs like a drum.

"Comin' after you, Terrell, comin' after you!" he shouted.

Like he was supposed to be scaring me or something. But just as he had his little salute ready for me, I had one ready for him. The patented Mile High Salute. I gave it after I scored the game's first touchdown, an eight-yard run not even six minutes into the game. In fact, our team spent a bunch of the first half saluting while we were racking up 24 first-half points on the way to a 24–14 halftime lead. But then we did get banged around. And we did get plenty scared.

In the second half, our offense got shut down and shut out. No matter what we tried, nothing worked. And the Steelers were starting to move the ball and gain some momentum, changing the flow of the whole game. All we wanted was the clock to run out on the game and the Steelers' season, but every time I looked at the scoreboard, the minutes and seconds seemed to be frozen. Meanwhile the Steelers points were building.

It was 24–14, Broncos, then 24–21, and in the end, what the game came down to was our third-and-six from our 15-yard line with 2:00 remaining. If we convert, we go to San Diego. We don't, Pittsburgh gets back the ball and probably winds up going to San Diego. So this one play meant the AFC Championship, a trip to the Super Bowl, and all the work we had put in all season long.

In the huddle, John Elway called a play not even in our playbook, "All Thunder." A big deal was made out of the fact that it wasn't in our playbook, but football is as much about common sense as talent. And "All" means that every receiver—including me, since I was lined up in the right flat—runs the same pattern. And "Thunder" means a five-yard hitch route. So every receiver is supposed to run a five-yard hitch route. Not too complex, is it?

The one receiver John spotted, and threw the ball to, was tight end Shannon Sharpe. Shannon bobbled the ball, the game, and the season, but in the end he held on—for 18 yards, a first down, and the AFC Championship. We were going to the Super Bowl! The Denver Broncos were Super Bowl–bound!

Suddenly, those same Steelers fans who had taunted us on the way into the stadium weren't so loud anymore. They were on their way home while we were making Three Rivers our playoff party headquarters. We whooped it up on the field, dancing around, celebrating like the champs we were. And the plane ride home was even more memorable. Talk about the friendly skies. These were the friendliest skies I had ever seen.

John Elway was sitting in the back of the plane with a smile that went from the window to the aisle seat. Shannon Sharpe was yelling that we were going to see Shamu the killer whale. And there was singing, plenty of singing. Everybody thought they were L.L. Cool J, singing "Going Back to Cali" from the soundtrack *Less Than Zero*:

> *I'm going back to Cali, Cali, Cali*
> *I'm going back to Cali*

The singing went on into the night. And as we celebrated, two things popped into my mind. All through the playoffs, I kept noticing how the number of teams playing each weekend shrank while the spotlight grew. When we played Jacksonville, eight teams were playing that weekend. Eight more the next weekend, when we went to Kansas City. Then it was down to four when we were in Pittsburgh. And now it was down to only two, the Denver Broncos and the Green Bay Packers. And all I wanted to know was, "Why not us?"—which I had been thinking ever since training camp?

The other thought popped into my mind when, out of the corner of my eye, I could see Alfred Williams partying it up. And I couldn't help thinking about a promise I had made to him, and to so many of my teammates, at the start of this whole playoff run. They had made good on their end of the bargain and now it was time for me to make good on mine.

They had gotten me there. It was time for me to help take them home.

Of course, two weeks later I did. In what many thought was the greatest Super Bowl ever played, we tore apart history and wrote our own. We beat the Packers 31–24 for the Broncos' first-ever Super Bowl win. The happiness and feeling of accomplishment I and the rest of my teammates felt after the game lasted the whole off-season, at least until we reported to training camp in July. To try to win the whole thing again.

16

THE MILE HIGH SALUTE

These days, just about everywhere I go, I see the Mile High Salute. It works like this. You assume the position of attention. You have your thumb and fingers extended and joined. You keep your hand and wrist on the same plane, not bent. You incline your forearm at 45 degrees. You hold your upper arm horizontal while your hand is at salute.

That's the Mile High salute. Now you should have it down. Everyone else seems to.

Not too long ago, I was in L.A. to tape a segment for *Arli$$*, the HBO sitcom. I got a nasty 5:45 A.M. wake-up call at my hotel, caught a ride over to the set, dragged into the studio, and just melted into a mushy little couch in my dressing room. Just as I was about to get a little shut-eye, the show's wardrobe designer popped into the room and introduced himself not by shaking my hand—the guy introduced himself by saluting me.

Soldier, let me tell you, I snapped right to attention. And Mile High saluted him right back.

And this is how I know it has become a coast-to-coast thing. A month or so before, I was in New York at Radio City Music Hall for ESPN's awards ceremony, the ESPY'S. I won an award for the "Best Performance Under Pressure" for the way I toted the rock during our Super Bowl win over the Packers. I marched up onstage, reached out to accept the award from comedian Jamie Foxx, and . . . got saluted.

I knew the Mile High Salute would be big, but I didn't realize it would be that big. I walk through airports these days— get saluted. I sit down in airport restaurants to have a little snack—get saluted. Heck, I go to any public men's room, unzip my fly, and as I start my rapid fire—get saluted. I would salute back, but, you know, I'm taking care of business.

I even noticed this thing catching on with other athletes early on, not long after I began using it. Last season, I'd be watching the New York Jets play and their running back Adrian Murrell, who now plays for the Arizona Cardinals, would be doing it. Or I'd be watching the Pittsburgh Steelers play, and I'd see linebacker Levon Kirkland doing it. I'd even get phone calls from some of my buddies saying, "Put on ESPN. A dude's out there doing your salute!"

And the first time I saw it, I was, like, "Hey, man, how dare you steal our salute!" But then, after a while, it was gratifying to see it had become so commonplace regardless of the sport. I'd see Pittsburgh Penguin Jaromir Jagr scoring and saluting. Same with all kinds of players in the NCAA hoops tournament, women and men. And every now and then, Colorado Rockies right-fielder Larry Walker would homer and salute. For a while there, you could barely watch a game, any kind of game, without seeing some player do it.

This thing had a life of its own. You would not believe the places it showed up: T-shirts, men's rooms, even on dates. One time I went out with one of my lady friends and when the night was over, she did something I never ever expected to see. This woman saluted me, Mile High style.

It's not like I sat at home during the off-season trying to think up something that would catch on like the Electric Slide. It just kind of came out of nowhere.

Each day during our 1997 training camp, after we wrapped up another day of drills in 90-plus temperatures, the Bronco running backs would gather together in a huddle, put their hands on top of each other's and shout, "RB's!" But the more we thought about it, the more we realized we're something more than just RB's because RB's are asked to do more than any other offensive player on the field. They have to run like backs, catch like receivers, block like linemen, do everything but throw the football, and sometimes they even do that on an option play. So in addition to learning the playbook, we were obsessed with coming up with a nickname for ourselves. It was like one big RB committee trying to figure something out.

There were so many different suggestions, so many different names, we must have gone through a thousand. One day we would shout, "Warriors!" and we'd be, like, "No, that's not real good, let's do something else," and it would be on to the next suggestion. Another day we would yell, "Special forces!" and we'd be, like, "No, that doesn't work either," and it would be on to something else.

And then we found a winner, yes indeedee. Soldiers. "Soldiers!" Perfect.

Like in war, football players are asked to do some crazy stuff, man. And even though it's violent and traumatic, you can't be scared. Like in war, you understand you can get knocked down and blown up. Like in war, there are going to be injuries. You're going to separate a few shoulders, blow out a few knees. That's football—combat without weapons. There's nothing nice about war, and there's nothing that's nice about football. And if you're scared—that's it, you're dead.

But then the RB's decided we wanted to be more than just "Soldiers." We wanted to be "No Limit Soldiers," just like the name of the rap song that my man Master P sang. We started to listen to that song incessantly at training camp.

> *We no limit soldiers*
> *I thought I told ya*
> *So b— get ya mind right*
> *I thought I told ya*

We believed there was no limit to what we soldiers could do. But for us it wasn't enough to find a nickname and sing about it. We wanted a little slogan, too. We wanted to come up with something that was catchy. Something that everybody—old people, young people, parents, kids—could do. So instead of throwing down our hands and shouting "No Limit Soldiers!" we decided to do something else, something more original. We decided to salute each other.

The salute was based on the instructions right out of the *Marine Corps Manual*. It was our way to recognize our teammates for all their hard work. It was something little, but it said a lot. Because to salute another person is one of the highest honors you can give them. It means, "You're putting in some work! You're a soldier, and I respect you! You're out there fighting, you're in the trenches with me! I salute you."

And we even discussed all kinds of nicknames for the salute. My teammate and fellow running back Vaughn Hebron wanted to call it the Soldier Salute. I told him that wouldn't work, couldn't work, and said, "People are going to be like what the hell's a 'Soldier Salute'?"

We needed to tie it in with the Broncos and the fans. We needed to come up with a nickname that tied in the fact that Denver is the Mile High city and the Broncos play in Mile High Stadium. Figured everybody knew what Mile High was. Wouldn't they know what the Mile High Salute was, too? We were about to find out.

We decided that the next time any one of us scored a touchdown, be it in a pre-season or regular-season game, we would assume the position of attention and salute each other. The first touchdown came in a pre-season game against the San Francisco 49ers. With 6:57 left in the first quarter of a game we won 31–17, I scored on an 11-yard run. After I got into the end zone, I turned, faced my team-mates, and saluted them.

Now that I think about it, it's kind of funny, because it seems like every year the team that wins the Super Bowl has some kind of shenanigans. The Chicago Bears started the Super Bowl Shuffle, the New York Giants started those Gatorade baths, the Green Bay Packers started the Lambeau Leap. And now there was the Mile High Salute.

For the first month of the season, we kept the salute under wraps, private, nobody's business but our own. We did it, we just refused to talk about it with reporters or fans. But then we thought about it and realized, "How cool it would be if 75,000-plus fans would be saluting right along with us!"

So in the days leading up to our game versus the Cincinnati Bengals at Mile High Stadium, on September 21, we told one reporter about it. Told him to pump it up in his paper, huge. And it was huge. We beat the Bengals 38–20, I ran for a franchise-record 215 yards, and the salute spread faster than a computer virus. The fans were doing it, the players were doing it, even our coach, Mike Shanahan, normally a pretty serious guy, was doing it.

In the post-game locker room, Mike took the football

that our defensive end Alfred Williams had used to score on his fourth-quarter 51-yard fumble return and handed it over to me. A game ball. Then, right smack in the middle of the locker room, Mike became the first Bronco coach in history to give the salute.

The man saluted me! The head coach! That was sweet.

The aftermath was pretty wild, too. For the first time I started seeing our teammates—the wide receivers, the tight ends, just about everyone—saluting like they were one of the original No Limit Soldiers. Even saw John Elway doing it. The way John did it was so messed up! His arm was way up in the air like some five-star general's, his head came up way too high, it was funny! But the man had the spirit.

Everyone did. Reporters started writing about it with the frequency they once wrote about my migraines. Newspapers were making full-page posters with the running backs outfitted in camouflage. The national networks—NBC, ESPN— started doing big pieces on it. Fans starting making banners that said, WE SALUTE THE DENVER BRONCOS.

The salute gave everybody a little extra motivation— remember, the only way to do it was to get into the end zone. I know I wanted to get there—like three, four times every game.

The whole team developed this soldier-type mentality, like the season was one big war game. Every city we had to go play in we named after a battleground. Kansas City was Vietnam, Pittsburgh was Iraq, everywhere was somewhere. We would pretend that we had missions in places only American soldiers had gone and when we returned to our homeland in Denver, we would look around and wonder how the soldiers came out. We would tally up the losses and tell each other, "Oh, man, we got four soldiers wounded. Didn't see the sniper out there. Didn't see the trap wire when I went over it. Man, it blew up everybody."

I couldn't get enough of the stuff, even outside the

locker room. One day I went shopping at the Cherry Creek Mall in Denver. I marched into F.A.O. Schwarz, saw this little G.I. Joe doll dressed in camouflage, wearing a forest-ranger hat, and said, "This is kind of cool, I must have this." It was like my own li'l Penny doll. It cost, like, 50 bucks, man, but this little dude was worth it. I brought him to work the next day and stuck him in my locker. I took a black felt-tip marker and drew in the number 30 on the brim of his hat. I sat him inside my locker and he stayed there all season. Liked him so much that, at the end of the season, I brought him home with me and displayed him on a shelf in my den. He's still sitting there—nice and quiet, the ideal roommate—as I write this. All year, nobody messed with him. He just sat upright, peacefully, his arms folded, a machine gun in his hand, just hanging out, making sure no crazy wars broke out.

None did, but there were minor ones. Some of the players around the league, on other teams, were not all that crazy about our salute. I remember when we played the Raiders in Oakland in October, their safety James Trapp knocked the hell out of me, jumped up and shouted, "Salute that!" And after they beat us, Raider wide receiver Tim Brown and their head coach Joe Bugel were saluting everyone they could. Bugel later said he was only—get this!—scratching his forehead. Yeah, right.

Now, I can understand why other teams and the NFL don't too much like touchdown celebrations. When you score a touchdown and you celebrate, that ticks off the whole other team. But to me, the Mile High Salute is so much classier, so much more understated, than those other touchdown celebrations. You're not jumping around, dancing everywhere, acting like a total fool.

I mean, I can't believe some of the celebration crap I see. Somebody makes a play and he's running around like he just made the play that won the Super Bowl. When you score a touchdown, you have to realize something. You're not the only one who made the play happen. You didn't score on your own.

And there's a fine line between appreciating the moment and your teammates and insulting the opposition. I think it's funny when our defensive end Alfred Williams does his little worm sack dance, and our defensive tackle Maa Tanuvasa does his Hawaiian sack dance, and our defensive end Neil Smith swings his post-sack baseball bat. That stuff is cool, funny. But sometimes a player can get a little carried away with taunting or acting like he just saved the world. To those players I would say, give the Mile High Salute a shot. It says a lot by doing a little.

As the season went on, as we accomplished our playoff missions in Kansas City and Pittsburgh, we managed to put little things into the Mile High Salute to spice it up. One time we let our hands shake uncontrollably as we were saluting. Another time all the running backs jumped in the air together as we saluted. It was wild, man.

For the Super Bowl, we knew we needed to come up with something different. So the day before the game, we're going through our walk-through practice at San Diego's Qualcomm Stadium and I thought we could do the salute, then stand at ease, just like they do in the military. I figured standing at ease means mission accomplished, you're free to go now. And that felt right for the big game.

And the guys were, like, "That's kind of cool." So we all practiced it—salute, stick your hands behind your back, spread your legs shoulder length, stand tall, at ease—and it was tight. We had ourselves a new Super Bowl Salute.

And when I got back to the team hotel later that day, I found out we also had a new song. There was a message waiting for me from the rapper Master P, the man himself. I could not believe it. Master P is huge, the founder of the No Limit record label. His albums *The Ghetto's Tryin' to Kill Me* and *TRUE* went gold, selling over 500,000. And his album *TRU 2 Da Game* went to the top of the R&B charts and hit double platinum. Not bad for a New Orleans boy who came from nothing.

We never had spoken before, but Master P called to tell me he had rewritten the song "No Limit Soldiers" to include lyrics about the Broncos, me and John Elway and Mike Shanahan. He was calling the song "Denver Broncos Soldiers." And I was, like, "P sat down to take his time to write a song for us?" I really appreciated that.

At the team meeting the night before the Super Bowl, I brought down the CD that Master P had made for us. When I hit the PLAY button, our team could not believe what they heard:

> *Master P on this dope*
> *Mike Shanahan be the coach*
> *Once the ref blows the whistle*
> *It's time to build the show, around*
> *Terrell Davis be running*
> *Shannon Sharpe keep gunning*
> *John Elway be humming*
> *That's why the ball's on the money . . .*
> *The Denver Broncos Soldiers,*
> *I thought I told ya,*
> *The Denver Broncos Soldiers*
> *I thought I told ya . . .*

We liked it so much, we brought the song with us to the Super Bowl and were playing it in the locker room over and over before we took the field. We wanted them to play it on the speakers as we took the field, but the NFL already had its music lineup set. No matter. Master P had done his job. He had come through for us. For the opening kick, man, we were all sauced up.

I'll tell you the other thing that got us all sauced up: our coach, Mike Shanahan. It never came out in the press, but the night before Super Bowl XXXII, Mike gathered our team together to show us some game film, which he always does the night before every game. Usually he'll show us the highlights of our team's previous week's game, from, typically, a nondescript wide-angle shot with no play-by-play voices on the tape.

But this time, he got a copy of the highlight tape that KUSA–Channel 9, Denver's NBC affiliate, had played on one of its Bronco specials. It was not just any highlight tape. It was an inspirational music video with all kinds of highlights from each one of our games, to the accompaniment of a Brian McKnight and Diana King duet, "When We Were Kings," a great song.

This video brought tears to your eyes. If you watched it—and it's so good, I now have a copy at home so that I can watch it anytime—you saw the type of camaraderie, the type of team work, the type of togetherness our team had. With the song on in the background, with the words matching the highlights like a music video, I was entranced, just staring at the screen. And I wasn't the only one like that. So was the rest of our team.

Normally when we're watching the previous week's game highlights, you hear a lot of comments from the team, people talking and laughing and not paying complete attention. But this time it was silence, not a word. The only thing you could hear was Brian McKnight and Diana King singing.

And when the long night has been fought and won
We'll stand in the sun . . .
And we will leave the world remembering
When we were kings

When the song ended and the highlights stopped, Mike turned off the tape and flicked on the light, and I knew everyone in the room felt the exact same way I did. I was ready to put on some pads and play the game. From that moment on, I knew we were going to be damn tough to beat in that game.

That's Mike, the essence of him. At all times, he knows which buttons to push, how to work his players, his coaches, the media, everyone who surrounds him. I've never played for another coach in the league, so of course I'm partial. But I can't imagine there's a better coach in the league. No other coach gets his team ready quite like this man.

This man is a perfectionist. Mike knows that if you don't do the little things in practice—hold on to every ball, run tight crisp patterns, use the proper techniques—then you won't do them in the game. He wants the best, demands the best, and gets it.

During Super Bowl week, people were asking our players if Mike was usually wound that tight. Hey, Mike wasn't any different on January 25 than he was on June 25, when training camp hadn't even started yet. The man is always intense. But he also is, as *Sports Illustrated* called him last season, The Mastermind.

In the past, when people have talked about great coaches, they haven't mentioned Mike's name in the same breath with guys like Bill Parcells and Jimmy Johnson and Mike Ditka and Mike Holmgren. Now maybe they will. I mean, going into the '98 season, there are only five active NFL coaches who have led their teams to Super Bowl wins. And last I checked, Mike Shanahan is one of them.

During the Super Bowl, after my first touchdown we didn't do the at-ease part of the Mile High Salute that we had worked on. But we did do it after the second two. And after the game-winning score, my one-yard touchdown run with 1:45 left in the game, our fullback Howard Griffith came running up to me and we did the Mile High Salute with emphasis. And stood at ease.

Our mission had been to get to the Super Bowl and win it. Now, finally, after a 16-game regular season and a four-game post-season, we were free to go. We had won the war.

I know this will sound crazy, but it's true. Of all the things I accomplished in 1997—setting a Super Bowl record with three rushing touchdowns, winning the Super Bowl MVP, rushing for a complete single-season NFL-record 2,331 yards, any record you can think of—being a founding father of the Mile High Salute means just as much as any of those things I did.

The day that we had the Super Bowl victory parade, when 650,000 fans filled the streets in downtown Denver and were saluting us like crazy, we were thrilled. This thing started out as something among me and my fellow running backs, and now our whole city, all our great fans, were giving it back to us.

People now ask me, "How are you going to celebrate touchdowns this year?" And I've got to be honest, I don't know. I didn't know going into the '97 season, and I sure as heck don't know going into the '98 season. What I do know is that the Mile High Salute is going to be one tough act to follow, no question about that. It's almost like if you put out a great movie, something like *Titanic*. How are you going to repeat that?

The thing about it is, the Mile High Salute will remain part of 1997, the year when there was so much greatness from start to finish. Now it's on to something else.

17

LOOKING AHEAD

Mr. Davis! Mr. Davis!"

I walked through the casino at the Mirage hotel; it was past three in the morning. I was trying to get back to my room, but people were grabbing me, touching me, waving paper and pens in my face, demanding my autograph as much as asking for it.

"Mr. Davis, sign this, please!"

I was, like, "Come on, man." It's wild. This is what my life has become. It's tough to go out in public without the people feeling like you belong to them. For 20-something years, I've played sports but haven't had to deal with the attention that can come along with it. It was always the other players—the Victor Deans, the Garrison Hearsts, the John Elways—who had to deal with it. Now it's all different.

Now I'm the man who has to deal with it and it's a huge adjustment. I'm having more trouble with that than with trying to stay at the top of my game because I don't view myself as a superstar. I'm just regular old Terrell, a normal person. But people don't treat me like that, not as often as they ask for autographs.

Now, I don't mind people asking me for autographs. But every day, every single day, you don't always feel like signing more and more autographs. I know people say, "That comes with the job." Well, do you always like your job? Probably not. Sometimes I just want to be left alone, like a normal civilian. So there are times when I shy away from the attention, and that might come off like I'm being rude. I'm trying to work on that, even though I know I'm not nearly as bad as some other athletes with autographs. (I remember reading somewhere that Bo Jackson, the former Royal outfielder and former Raider running back, once had a sign bolted to his front door that said ABSOLUTELY NO AUTOGRAPHS: THANK YOU.)

But that is partly why it has been, and continues to be, such a difficult adjustment. I'm used to living my own life, going to the mall when I want, going to eat when I'm hungry, just jumping into my car and driving to a basketball or hockey game. Now I've got to contemplate everything I do, every place I go, think about whether or not I want to leave the quiet of my home.

For me to go out now, I have to be in the mood to deal with the kinds of attention that usually goes to supermodels and superstars. But I'm figuring if my career goes the way I want it to, the yards and the attention are only going to keep on growing and growing. The more attention you get, the better you must be doing as an athlete. So as much as I don't always like it, there's a part of me that hopes I'll be Michael-Jordan-mobbed for the next 10 years. That'll mean I'm the best in my field, the best *on* the field, which is more important to me.

But you know what? The more I'm around it, the wiser I get, the better I'm learning how to deal with it. And I tell you what has really helped: watching John Elway, and how he handles the spotlight. I observe just about everything he does—how he talks to the media, how he acts with the fans, how he deals with the public—so that when I'm in that same position, I can handle it as well as No. 7.

Deep-down inside, I know it's a burden on him, but he doesn't convey that. He makes it like he enjoys it, like he's a rookie and it's all so new to him. I cannot tell you how glad I am he has decided to stick around for this final season. That means I'll continue having a great quarterback to learn, and take handoffs, from.

What's next for me? My goals now are more long term than short term. I could have a year like last year, be satisfied, then come out and flop. With long-term goals, I've got to work harder and harder every year. And believe me, if you had seen me go through my off-season workouts last spring, you would know that I will work harder and harder every year.

My first long-term goal? After writing this book, I want to rewrite the Bronco record book. By the time I'm through, by the time I hang up my Nikes, I want to own every Bronco rushing record there is. The first one I'm taking a run at? The franchise rushing record. Floyd Little gained 6,323 yards, and going into my fourth NFL season, I had 4,405. Watch out, Mr. Little, I'm coming after you, and anyone else in the Bronco rushing record book.

The way I'm figuring it, if my name is all over the record book, that will also say that I've played a long time and done it at a high level. To me, that's very important. I'm thinking some people might look at me now and say, "Three years in the league, who cares?" I mean, how many years has John Elway been in the league? Fifteen? And Emmitt Smith and Barry Sanders? Eight and nine. Longevity, as much as the championship rings, is the mark of a champion.

Eventually I would like to be able to walk off the field at the new Mile High Stadium our organization is pushing for and say, "Hey, I played ten years with the Broncos, and it's been a great ten years, and I've been to four Super Bowls, and I consider myself the luckiest man on the face of this earth."

I'll tell you the other thing I look at now, aside from long-term goals. The Super Bowl. You think about it, the great players have done memorable things in the championship games. That puts them at a whole different level. I always look at Buffalo Bill running back Thurman Thomas, who lost four Super Bowls, and I say, "In terms of recognition, Thurman is not where he should be—just because he has not won a championship."

If Thurman had won even one Super Bowl, he would be compared to the greatest backs of all time. Now, a lot of people just forget about him because he never got over the hump of winning a championship game. It's almost like he's an afterthought, like he doesn't get the credit he deserves. I never want that to happen to me.

The other thing that keeps me stoked about the future is defending our championship, the thing the Broncos worked so hard for so long to earn. People ask me all the time whether the Broncos can repeat this season. All I can tell you is, the feeling around our locker room is that we are meant to be champions. It's a contagious feeling, winning. When people come here to play for the Broncos, the expectations of winning are extremely high. They've been high from the time Dan Reeves coached here; and since Mike Shanahan has been here, they've been even higher. Mike demands a lot of his players, and he forces the players to demand a lot of themselves. Now it's to the point in Denver where anything less than winning the Super Bowl just won't do. You have to feel that way. If you believe in something, have a strong conviction about something, I'm thinking you can't be denied.

Anyhow, if I can become a fixture in the Bronco record book, play a long time, and help run Denver into and through a few more Super Bowls, I should be able to have the kind of career no one ever could have imagined for me, including myself. I believe all these goals are going to keep me motivated. Because when I finish playing for the Broncos, I don't want anybody to wear No. 30. Ever again. I want to be viewed around Colorado, and the football world, the way John Elway is viewed around here. I want my name to be synonymous with the Broncos, the way John's is today. All that—that's what keeps my fires stoked.

Then, if that's not enough motivation, there's another little story, something that just always seems to stick out in my mind. I happened to be in New York last spring when the Yankees played their home opener. The Yankees invited the U.S. women's hockey team that had won a gold medal in Nagano to be their guests, and Joe DiMaggio was to throw out the first pitch. At one point before the game, the women's hockey team and DiMagggio found themselves standing together. Katie King, one of the hockey players, introduced herself and said, "Our coach always used your name to motivate us, Mr. DiMaggio."

DiMaggio asked how so and King told him, "Before our games leading up to the Olympics, when we'd go from city to city, he'd always tell us to make sure to have a 'Joe DiMaggio day.'"

"And what," the old man said with a grin, "is a 'Joe DiMaggio day'?"

King told him. "He said that one time, late in the season after the Yankees clinched the pennant, somebody wanted to know why you'd played so hard that day, in a game that really didn't mean anything. And you said there might be people in the ballpark that day who might only ever see you play once, and you owed them your best."

So every Sunday I believe I have to prove to myself to

all the people watching, whether they're watching me for the first time or the hundredth, that I'm as good as any back in the league. Every Sunday I'll be out there trying to play the best I can.

It's not like I invented a cure for cancer or won the Nobel Prize. I mean, if you define yourself through football, then you're a pretty shallow person. Me, I do play football, but I intend to do a lot more than that.

I've already gotten involved with Turnabout, a day shelter for the homeless at the St. Francis Center in Denver. I've visited there and brought the people all kinds of goodies—T-shirts and sweatshirts and caps. But I know that's not near enough. I'm probably as guilty as anyone else of not giving as much time as I should to go visit the kids at the recreation centers, or the sick kids at the hospitals. I know it's easy to say, "Yeah, I'm going to get more involved," but I'm telling you I will be, you watch. I want the community to depend on me the way the Broncos do.

I've already started my Terrell Davis Salutes the Kids Foundation, and that's really going to help. We're going to provide kids with computers, tutors, athletic equipment, the things they need to have a better childhood. My mother and brothers are going to be involved so we can tackle more assignments and help more children. That's where everything begins. That's when people need to be reached most, when they're children.

I might even be able to give my brothers some more work, in addition to the foundation. By the time I'm through with the Broncos, I want to be able to go from running a football to running a business, and the thing I'm thinking about most is a construction company. It's something I've always wanted to do, own a construction company. I still don't know whether it would specialize in drywalling, cementing, plumbing, framing, or whatever. But I do know that I want to be a part of it.

I recognize I'll have to go to some type of trade school, maybe do some interning somewhere. Mom's always telling me and my brothers that before we buy any business, we sure better know what we're getting into. I know I have to do a lot of stuff before I buy anything, but I'm ready for it. I was hoping to get some type of an internship with a construction company after we won Super Bowl XXXII. But then there were so many commercial shoots and photo shoots and TV shoots that, before I knew it, it was summertime. Time to get back to training camp.

After the 1998 season, though, I'm shooting to line up that internship. I want to get involved, go watch people work, get me my own tool belt, hard hat, work boots, messed-up T-shirt and ripped-up jeans. I want to learn everything there is to learn, then try to buy my way into a partnership with an already established construction company. Once I buy in, I would love to be able to bring in my brothers and friends. Of course, they would have to be trained for it. But I know they could and would be. My oldest brother, Joe, he does great plumbing work. A company like the one I envision would be a great opportunity for him, and me.

The other business I'm thinking about getting into? Cars. Pricey cars. Like I said, I've studied John, watched the way he has acted, and if the business is good enough for him, it's good enough for me. Whereas he sells Fords, I would like to sell higher-end cars, European cars—Mercedes, BMWs. As of the spring, I hadn't talked to John about the car business. But believe me, I'm planning to.

I'm also planning on having a wife and kids in the hopefully not-too-distant future. That's the one thing in my life still missing. I definitely see myself finding a Mrs. 30, getting married, becoming a father, building a family around me to share all this with. I think about that more than people realize. These days I'll come home to an empty house—no wife, no kids—and it's like, "Dang! I'm having the greatest time of my life and no one's here to share it with me."

And after our games are over, I'll see my teammates' wives waiting for them, with all their little sons and daughters hugging and kissing their daddies. A lot of times when I see that, it makes me feel empty, like I'm missing something. I want to be able to bring all my little T.D.s to my games. I want to take them trick-or-treating on Halloween. I want to take them on Easter egg hunts. But I won't do it without a wife. I've always told myself that I'm going to get married, then have kids—not the other way around. It's tough enough to raise children. It's even tougher to do as a single parent. I'm not going to have any kids wondering and asking, "Where's Daddy?" But I am determined to have kids before I'm 30. Because as an NFL running back, my body's so beat up that when I'm 30, it'll be like I'm really 50. I need to be able to pick up my children, to be able to take them to the park and play with them there. And I need to be around to see my children's children. So the way I figure it, 30 would be the perfect age to have children.

Other than that, though, I have just about everything I could want. This is one incredible ride. I don't want to jinx myself, but I can't even wait until tomorrow, because things seem to get better every day. It's to the point now where it's hard to believe everything that has and is going on in my life. If I were to jump outside my body and get a chance to read my life story, my autobiography, I would say, "Man, that's amazing. I've never heard, seen, or read a story like this—never."

People come up to me all the time now and ask for training tips, eating tips, survival tips. Essentially, inspirational tips. All I can tell them is, it's a mind-set, a resolve-type issue. I've always felt that you can do anything you want, anything, and I really mean that. In this world, there's nobody who can tell you what you can and cannot do.

You have a choice in life, to do it the hard and right way, or the easy and wrong way. The choice is yours, not anyone else's. It's so easy to do wrong, to take the easy way out. I've seen it happen right in front of me. Hell, I've done it myself. When I was in school, I didn't always put in the time and effort I would have needed to get the grades I wanted. But you know what? If you want something bad enough, there's nothing holding you back.

I believe The Man Upstairs, He gives you a lot of challenges, a lot of things that make you wonder, "Why is this happening to me?" But all He's really doing is building character. Life would be so easy for you to go through if you had everything your way. But when you go through a lot of setbacks and a lot of obstacles, it builds you as a person and makes you appreciate the things you learn even more. With what I've been through in the past, there's a lot of things that I look at now and say, "I can't believe this is happening." Every day is a dream. Every year that I come back to the Broncos for another year of power rushes and power naps, the dream is living.

Unfortunately, the way this world works, it's not going to continue forever. You don't have to tell me; I know that. It's just like the situation with the Dallas Cowboys, who earlier this decade won three Super Bowls in four years. One day they're on top of the football world and the next they're talking about when we were kings.

Just like it happened with them, eventually it's going to start crumbling with me, and everything is going to be confusion and mayhem, and it's going to be a wild, wild day. But until then? Don't kill my dream. It's still in motion.

ACKNOWLEDGMENTS

Of those who performed like offensive linemen, in the background without much fanfare, the authors would like to give special thanks to Neil Schwartz, who envisioned and believed in this book from start to finish; Mike Shanahan, for bringing Terrell and a Super Bowl champion and the opportunity for this book to Denver; John Elway, who can write almost as well as he throws; Basil Kane, who found a buyer when it didn't seem like there was one; Mauro DiPreta, who believed in this book when other editors didn't; Kateree Davis, Joe Davis, James Davis, Reggie Davis, Bobby Davis, Terry Davis—the family who shared their time and their memories; Ryan McKibben, Dennis Britton, and Neal Scarbrough of the *Denver Post*, who took the time to help make this project happen; Mitch Albom, who showed us the way; Rick Reilly, who told us the way; Cindy Marshall, an assistant and a friend; Patrick Falencik and the guys over at Discount Used Computers, who saved our book and our sanity; John Ingold and Justin George, who were "A" students all the way.

Thanks also to: Chris Tama and Wayne Yetter of Novartis, people who could get rid of any headache; Phil Knight, Bill Kellar, Greg Young, and Nancy Benoit of Nike, who fit the glass slippers on the feet; Bill Phillips and Rick Anderson of EAS (Experimental Applied Sciences), who have been huge; the NFL, the best league in sports; Campbell's Soup, which is "M'm! M'm! Good!"; SONY; Pat Bowlen, The Man; Frank White, Corey White, Reginald White, and Rashon White, who knew "Boss Hogg" way back when; Mark Watson, a great poet and even better companion; Dorian Leniar and Curtis Waters, lifelong friends; Vic Player, Lincoln High School's former football coach; Tony Jackson, Lincoln's former offensive coordinator; Jim Saccomano, Paul Kirk, and Richard Stewart, who were quick with numbers and help; Jordon Schefter, Mr. FedEx; CBS, ESPN, ABC, NBC, FOX-TV, and TNT; Thomas George; John McClain; Vic Carucci; Chris Havel; the boys at 930 Church; Don Kubit; Sam Jean; Cary Fabrikant; Wendell Bass; Ken Ready; Jennifer Kirchmeier; Camille Kesler; Dick Bestwick; Preston Hughes IV; Greg O'Neal; Chantal and the Rug Rats; Gail Boyer; Dorothy Woodland; Zella Price; Claude Felton; NAS; the Fugees; FUBU; and Giorgio Armani.

—*Terrell Davis and Adam Schefter*

Adam, I know this is your first book—for a rookie, you're an All-Pro.

Mike Shanahan, Bobby Turner, and all my coaches and teammates—you guys are the best!

—*T.D.*

Thanks, Terrell, for being a great subject and an even greater guy.

—*A.S.*